LET EVENING COME

JANE KENYON

Let Evening Come

SELECTED POEMS

BLOODAXE BOOKS

ISBN: 978 1 85224 697 6

First published 2005 by
Bloodaxe Books Ltd,
Eastburn,
South Park,
Hexham,
Northumberland NE46 1BS.

www.bloodaxebooks.com
For further information about Bloodaxe titles
please visit our website and join our mailing list
or write to the above address for a catalogue.

Supported using public funding by
**ARTS COUNCIL
ENGLAND**

Digital reprint of the 2005 edition.

ACKNOWLEDGEMENTS

All the poems in this selection are drawn from Jane Kenyon's *Collected Poems* (Graywolf Press, 2005). With the exception of 'Woman Why Are You Weeping', which was first collected in *A Hundred White Daffodils: Essays, Interviews, The Akhmatova Translations, Newspaper Columns and One Poem* (Graywolf Press, 1999), all these poems were published in *Otherwise: New & Selected Poems* (Graywolf Press, 1996); 'Woman Why Are You Weeping' and 'The Sick Wife' are late poems which have been added here at the end of the new poems first collected in *Otherwise*.

Twenty Poems of Anna Akhmatova, translated from the Russian by Jane Kenyon and Vera Sandomirsky Dunham, was first published by Eighties Press/All Press in 1985, and reprinted in *A Hundred White Daffodils*.

'Everything I Know About Poetry' is a series of notes for a lecture delivered in 1991 at a literary conference in Enfield, New Hampshire. The interview with David Bradt was recorded at Eagle Pond Farm in March 1993, and first published in *The Plum Review* in 1996. Both these pieces are reprinted from *A Hundred White Daffodils*.

Joyce Peseroff's introduction is reprinted from *Simply Lasting: Writers on Jane Kenyon* (Graywolf Press, 2005), edited by Joyce Peseroff. Donald Hall's 'Ghost in the House' conflates a memoir of the same name from *Simply Lasting* with part of his Afterword to *Otherwise*. His memoir was originally commissioned, in 1999, for a book about depression.

For permission to reprint any of the poetry and prose in this book, please contact: Graywolf Press, 2402 University Avenue, Suite 203, Saint Paul, Minnesota 55114, USA.

PHOTOGRAPHS: *5:* William Abranovicz, 1993. *10:* Donald Hall, 1990. *16:* Ken Williams, 1993. *27:* Donald Hall, 1990. *29:* Robyn Brown, 1988. *168a:* Robyn Brown (Jane Kenyon with Gus), 1988. *169b:* Robyn Brown (with Ada), 1988.

CONTENTS

Introduction

Jane Kenyon was an artist at the height of her power when, six months after a bone marrow transplant, she died of leukemia in April 1995. Her poems, those 'brief musical cries of the spirit', moved thousands who heard them, and thousands more who read the four volumes praised by reviewers. Bill Moyers interviewed her for the Emmy Award winning documentary, *A Life Together*. Composers set her work to music. She wrote newspaper columns for and about her neighbors in Wilmot, New Hampshire, as well as essays on gardening and mountain climbing. She visited the Bennington Writing seminars to read and talk about her favorite poets. Her verse grew ever more discursive, ambitious, and complex. That there will be no more writing by Jane Kenyon is one of the terrible losses that might have been otherwise.

I first met Jane Kenyon in 1972, one of two poets accepted that year as Junior Fellows in the newly-minted University of Michigan Society of Fellows. The program offered artists and scholars three luxurious years of thinking and writing, with few responsibilities or requirements other than residence in Ann Arbor. In the 1970s Jane's hair was straight, and she wore black-framed glasses she would later exchange for contact lenses. But her voice was the same modulated music you can hear in her later readings. I was invited to join her workshops with Gregory Orr, which had started the year before; she and Donald Hall took me to a Michigan football game; we attended Society dinners (Don was a Senior Fellow) and campus poetry readings; we became friends.

A year after I returned to Massachusetts, Don and Jane moved to New Hampshire. I might have been the only soul within a hundred miles, other than Don, she'd known from her Ann Arbor days; lucky for me, a two-hour drive brought Jane to Cambridge for bookstores, tacos and beer, or me to the farmhouse for generous meals and hours of talk. She nicknamed us the country mouse and the city mouse, though I – a native New Yorker, and a fine example of urban provincialism – was drawn to her sophistication and perfect manners. Together we worked on *Green House*, a literary magazine we'd planned while still in Michigan. We divided editorial duties, and educated ourselves in the details of layout, production, and distribution. We published friends and discovered strangers; our goal was to provide a forum for poets who didn't know each other, and whose work could not usually be found in the same magazine, to find common readers. Over three years of the magazine's existence, we tested and refined our notions of what made a good poem. When her first collection, *From Room to Room*, was published in 1978, Jane Kenyon was firmly part of a New England literary community.

Jane was witty, inventive, fun. She discovered that lengths of gutter made perfect pans for baking French bread. She patiently leveled and set in sand the large brick patio patterned behind her house. She also told me how much she enjoyed reading ads for extravagant handbags in the Sunday *New York Times*, and once we went to Bloomingdale's in Chestnut Hill for a free cosmetic consultation and makeover. When we met at the Mall of New Hampshire, halfway between Lexington and Wilmot, to exchange poems and news, Jane bought earrings and scarves in fine fabrics. Later we chose books for my daughter and her five grandchildren, including *The Stupids Die*, a title she adored, and the Margaret Wise Brown's *The Runaway Bunny*, whose theology – 'It's like the love of God!' – made her weep. She loved Mahler and Motown, Dutch paintings and poker-playing dog placemats, Beethoven and Mel Brooks, lotions and baths.

Once, while Jane was working on *Twenty Poems of Anna Akhmatova*, she took me to Vera Sandomirsky Dunham's home on Long Island. Jane was choosing, with Vera's advice, several more poems to translate. I remember thick black volumes of Akhmatova's work like a complete edition of the *Oxford English Dictionary*, and how Vera read aloud several poems in Russian. I also remember Vera Dunham's oft-repeated, 'This is impossible! It cannot be done!' after her reading: no poem in English, she believed, could properly render Akhmatova's sound, or her intricate form. For a while it did seem as if that day she would go no further. Then she sat with Jane, providing a literal translation, answering Jane's questions concerning connotation and tone, and explaining historical details such as what the 'tree-lined drive' in 'Tale of the Black Ring' might look like. The Dunhams' guest bathroom was scarlet, and before we left, Jane nudged me to notice Vera's full-length Russian sable coat in the hall closet. Later, Jane was ambitious to translate Akhmatova's masterpiece *Requiem*, but, whether because of Vera's husband's illness, or Vera's, or her own, she never did. Perhaps she knew she had learned what her master had to teach her: a precise way of describing great emotional intensity through imagery as plain as a white stone in a deep well, or a winter glove put on the wrong hand.

If I had to pick one perfect, exemplary day I spent with Jane, it would be in late spring, 1993. She was visiting the college where I taught to take part in a 20th-anniversary reading for Alice James Books. I joined her that morning at Symphony Hall (she and Don had season tickets for the Boston Symphony Orchestra's Thursday open rehearsal). Over and over the singer repeated her gorgeous aria; Jane's pleasure was palpable. After the rehearsal we had lunch – probably in the Cinderella restaurant that served students delicious home-cooked pasta by day and became a tony boite at night – on our way to the original Filene's Basement, where Jane sorted through bins of sassy shoes, hunting for bargains. Then came the reading, old poems and new ones from *Constance*, which would be published later that year. It's possible that she read 'No Steps', and I remember her saying that she'd written it partly for the pleasure of getting 'ziplock plastic bag' into the language of a poem. An audience of students, faculty, fellow readers, and Boston friends filled the room – intent on every word – applauded, and bought books.

The tone of those books was often bleak. Jane enjoyed the things of this world, but there's a terrifying longing for the void in her poems – desire for oblivion, for nada, paralysis, immobility, or effacement in sleep's 'frail wicker coracle'. The newborn welcomed by shouts in 'Caesarian' is shocked by light and noise. Entrance into the world is disordered (outside in, inside out), an introduction to the abyss. Kenyon's poems interrogate the abyss: why live, when life is suffering? Like Akhmatova, Kenyon knows trouble, the shadow between 'love's tense joys and red delights'.

Yet throughout the body of her work, things – a stone warmed by sun, a wood thrush, a clothespin, a long gray hair, hay bales, rushing water, peonies – answer existential doubt and dread. Whether gifts of the Holy Ghost, or 'thoughts /in an unconflicted mind', they are preceptors. Kenyon's poems are not didactic but they always show us where to look. In 'Depression in Early Winter', it's at a crescent of bare ground; in 'Portrait of a Figure Near Water' it's a stone trough; in 'Let Evening Come', it's everything. 'Go to the pine to learn from the pine,' Bashō wrote four centuries ago; Kenyon's work is a 20th-century response. What adds pressure to these poems is the landscape in which so many of these objects reside. Fields, woods, ponds and streams, hayrick, shed, farmhouse, inn, general store – Kenyon describes a rural life that is fading fast. The whip-poor-will, dispossessed by men making hay, may be dispossessed for good, if fields become real estate. Kenyon's poems argue for the preservation of an ecology as strongly as anything by Gary Snyder, if more subtly. For how can we give the world our steady attention if its natural objects disappear?

Man-made objects, other than domestic ones – the snowplow, school clothes and satchels, the wineglass weary of holding wine – often conduct disquiet and grief rather than joy. Even music and books – the Chopin and Nabokov that pained her father, and the Keats she loves but cannot bear to read – may be charged with suffering. Surely there is something of Wordsworth in Kenyon's gaze. Wordsworth saw nature's beauty as proof of God's hand in creation; by delighting in the scent of roses, plush of moss, play of sky and clouds, man learns to love his creator. But Kenyon doesn't write just about beautiful things. The hen's foot is 'reptilian', snow and rain can be violent, the mouse leaves behind its shit and smell. So why this feeling of joy when she writes, 'Now is her time to thrive'? Whether Kenyon's eyes are on the sparrow or the skunk, we are persuaded to invest them with complete attention, as Kenyon's words – and possibly the Word – have. We may live in the abyss, God may be distant, indifferent, or dead, there maybe no earthly reason to lift an arm from a chair – all the same, Kenyon does the work of discovering all that this world is made of.

She didn't much like cities or suburbs, places where it was possible to overhear and yet avoid a neighbor's pain. Jane didn't avoid anything. The intimacy of voice in a Jane Kenyon poem erases the line between her vision and the reader's. The structure of her sentences reveals a mind in motion – a strategy learned from Elizabeth Bishop, but employed differently. Kenyon, avoiding nothing, doesn't insist on conclusion. The ellipse – something she admired in Louis Simpson's poems – indicates the end of one thought before it flows into another. Kenyon's poems seem lifted directly from the poet's consciousness.

She once described writing poetry as taking off her clothes in front of everyone, which implies exhibitionism, seduction, frankness, and bravery. These are qualities necessary to a voice essentially alone, confronting space both infinite and eternal. One needs quiet, solitude, and belief in the importance of perception in order to measure the progress of a beating heart.

'One of the functions of poetry is to keep the memory of people and places and things and happenings alive,' Kenyon said to Bill Moyers during an interview. This is true of collections like this one as well. I recognise that any volume about Jane Kenyon must be incomplete, since even as I type these words, someone is writing a paper, an article, a review, or a poem in response to Kenyon's life and work. That is both joy and pain, as is the fact that I can no longer speak to Jane, though she still speaks to me – and to each reader – through words that are 'simply lasting'.

DONALD HALL

Ghost in the House

Jane Kenyon was born in Ann Arbor, Michigan, 23 May 1947. With her older brother, she grew up in a house of freelancers. Her father Reuel played piano all his life. He played *le hot jazz* in Europe as a young man and later toured with American dance bands. (He jammed with Bix Beiderbecke in 1930.) Settled down with his family, he gave lessons and played in bars and clubs. Jane's mother Polly had sung with orchestras in night clubs and, when her children were born, turned seamstress and teacher of sewing. The family lived on the outskirts of town, on a dirt road opposite a working farm, in a house crowded with pictures, books, and music. Jane went to a one-room school through the fourth grade.

During junior high school she began to write poems. Witter Bynner's translations from the Chinese were an early model. At the University of Michigan, where she majored first in French and then in English, she won a Hopwood Award. We met in 1969, courted in 1971, and married in 1972. In 1975, with Jane's encouragement, I quit my university job and we moved to Eagle Pond Farm, my family's place in New Hampshire. Here, she read and reread certain authors with excitement and devotion – Keats to begin with, most strikingly Akhmatova (whom she translated with Vera Sandomirsky Dunham), later Chekhov and Bishop. Her poetry gathered resonance and beauty as she studied the art of the luminous particular. 'The natural object' – she liked to quote Pound – 'is always the adequate symbol.'

Her readers are aware of Jane's struggles with depression – and also of her joy in the body and the creation, in flowers, music, and paintings, in hayfields and a dog. We had almost twenty years together at Eagle Pond Farm, engaged separately in a common enterprise, commonly loving land and house and church and friends.

Jane died of leukemia on 22 April 1995. The disease was diagnosed in January of 1994, in a virulent form; chemotherapy could induce remission but could not sustain it, and only a bone marrow transplant (BMT) offered hope for extended life. In Seattle, a new marrow from an anonymous donor was infused on November 18th.

Jane was discharged on December 20th, and we returned to New Hampshire with good hope on 24 February 1995.

For six weeks her blood counts improved. She was weak and impaired, as expected after a BMT; it would take a year for her to recover. She could read little, and she could not write because an anti-rejection drug disabled her fingers. Nevertheless, she began to think about what poems to include in *Otherwise* as she underwent the transplant. She intended to complete the book as her strength came back. But on 11 April 1995, bloodwork revealed that leukemia had returned. There was nothing to do, and she died eleven days later, at home in our bed as she wished.

We were married for twenty-three years. When I first met her, Jane was moody. Laughing extravagantly with other student poets, she was funny, outrageous, and smart. Then she would go silent, withdraw, her mouth curved down, her forehead knotted. Most of the time when she felt low, she kept to herself. She consulted a university doctor who prescribed a drug that appeared to deepen her depression. When we were first married, she spent two years in psychoanalytical therapy, which did not cure depression but which helped her to interpret feelings, to avoid the emotional erratum slips that most of us should wear on our foreheads: 'For 'compassion' read 'anger' throughout.'

Three years after we married, Jane and I moved to the isolation of our New Hampshire farmhouse, largely at Jane's urging. For twenty years we inhabited a double solitude at Eagle Pond, thriving in cohabitation and in boundaries. Each leaving her/his separate hive of writing, we could meet in the kitchen for another coffee, mid-morning, without speaking; we would pat each other's bottoms. In our silence, we were utterly aware of each other's presence. In our devotion to poetry and each other, our marriage was intimate and content.

And nothing is simple. By temperament, I was impatient, always eager, as Jane said, for 'the next thing, the next thing'. Often she sank into speechless discontent while I remained energetic. Then in her poems I encountered depression that was more than moodiness. Old harness in the barn suggested itself a noose. There were poems of blankness and lethargy:

> I had to ask two times
> before my hand would scratch my ear.

In another she wrote:

> ...The days are bright
> and free, bright and free.
>
> Then why did I cry today
> for an hour, with my whole
> body, the way babies cry?

Eleven years after we married, Jane was diagnosed with bipolar mood disorder.

> ...the soul's bliss
> and suffering are bound together
> like the grasses...

She was never delusional; her mania was notable but God never telephoned her. On the other hand, her depression ranged from deep sadness to agony, and Jane was more frequently depressed than manic.

Psychiatrists have documented the high incidence of bipolarity among artists. Writers are the most bipolar – and among writers, poets. See 'Manic-Depressive Illness and Creativity' by Kay Redfield Jamison in *Scientific American* (February 1995). One percent 'of the general population suffer from manic-depression'. Jamison cites figures for mood disorder in artists, depending on different models of sampling, that go upward from thirty-eight percent.

No one can induce bipolarity in order to make poems. Does the practice of the art exacerbate a tendency? Surely for the artist the disorder is creative in its manic form – excitement, confidence, the rush of energy and invention. Maybe DNA perpetuates bipolarity because mania or hypomania benefits the whole tribe, inventing the wheel and Balzac's *Cousine Bette*, while depression harms only the depressive and those close to the depressive.

Ten years after we married, I watched Jane lower into the blackest place. She had been a principle caregiver for her father, and she was with him when he died. She stayed up all night with him when morphine confused him, and with her mother tended him twenty-four hours a day. The cancer that wasted him, his collapse in mind and tissue, commanded her asleep or awake. In 1982, six months after the death, we drank a beer one night in the small town of Bristol. As we drove back, Jane sank under a torment and torrent of wild crying. At home she curled on the sofa in the fetal position and wept for three days. I wanted to hold and comfort her, as I had earlier done when she was low, but now I could not touch her. If I touched her, she would want to scream.

She spoke little, in gasps, but she told me that she was not angry at me, that she loved me, that her despair had nothing to do with me. It was heartbreaking not to touch her, not to be able to give comfort. Doubtless my anxious presence across the room was another burden. I understood and believed that I was not responsible for her melancholia. In later returns of her sickness, she continued to worry that I would misinterpret her feelings. She persuaded two doctors to tell me that her depression was caused by the chemistry of her brain, that it was endogenous and unrelated to our life together.

That first black time, she gradually stopped weeping and her mood rose slightly. She saw our internist, who recognised clinical depression and prescribed drugs; I'm not sure which drug he began with but it must have been tri-cyclic. The Prozac class of drugs (which didn't help Jane) was not yet available. For advice on treatment, our doctor spoke with Dr Charles Solow, head of psychiatry at Dartmouth-Hitchcock Hospital. Later, Jane visited Dr Solow regularly, and relied on him for treatment until she died. He prescribed a variety of drugs, and talked with her continually – kind, supportive, sympathetic. Jane was medicated most of the rest of her life. She kept wanting to survive without pharmaceutical help, and in 1992 tried the experiment of going naked. A precipitate plunge returned her to medication.

In 'Having It Out with Melancholy', she makes a stanza:

> Elavil, Ludiomil, Doxepin,
> Norpramin, Prozac, Lithium, Xanax,
> Wellbutrin, Parnate, Nardil, Zoloft.
> The coated ones smell sweet or have
> no smell; the powdery ones smell
> like the chemistry lab at school
> that made me hold my breath.

The tri-cyclic Doxepin helped her for three years, the longest stretch without a deep trough. During these years she had her ups and downs, she was sad and she was gay, but Doxepin appeared to prevent deep depression. As she inhabited a fragile comfort, she could work on her poems. Then her body learned how to metabolise the drug and she needed larger doses, until it was no longer safe to increase the dose.

This drug, like others, gave her a dry mouth, but the side effects were not miserable. Some drugs did nothing for her, or reduced the intensity of orgasm, or included side effects nasty enough to disqualify them. When she was manic in 1984, she took Lithium, which she hated. Lithium is known to suppress creativity. After that year, she was never manic for long episodes. Often she dosed daily on a combination of drugs – Wellbutrin maybe, a tri-cyclic or two, a trace of Lithium. Another drug that helped was an old MOA-inhibitor, Nardil, which kept her from depression for almost a year, but limited her sleep so much that she became exhausted and had to stop taking it. Despite her energy and relief from dolor, I didn't like some side effects of Nardil, nor did her closest friends. She seemed much as she seemed in mania: dogmatic, combative, sometimes querulous, abrasive sometimes – without her characteristic alertness to the feelings of others. But Nardil held depression off. She described herself in a section of 'Having It Out with Melancholy':

WOOD THRUSH

High on Nardil and June light
I wake at four,
waiting greedily for the first
notes of the wood thrush. Easeful air
presses through the screen
with the wild, complex song
of the bird, and I am overcome

by ordinary contentment.
What hurt me so terribly
all my life until this moment?
How I love the small, swiftly
beating heart of the bird
singing through the great maples;
its bright, unequivocal eye.

With Dr Solow's help, Jane avoided deepest depression much of the time, but its misery lurked at the edges of her daily life, and sometimes sprang from the shadows. I remember Jane on the bathroom floor banging her head against toilet and pipes. Another time she arrived trembling after driving back from Concord: she

21

had fought all the way the impulse or desire to drive off the road into a boulder or a stone wall. And I remember a terrible Christmas Day, when I gave her as usual too many presents, each of which depressed her further. Someone who is stupid, bad, ugly, fat, and hateful does not deserve presents; gifts mocked her. After this bout lapsed, the presents I had given her always retained a tint of misery. The counterpart can be true: Recollections of a manic experience may cheer you up, even though you know that the joy was endogenous and ended in depression.

Despite her thoughts about hanging herself with a horse's harness, despite her fear of driving into walls, I did not think that Jane would kill herself. Maybe her treatment kept her from the extremes that lead to suicide. Surely her Christianity helped: She knew that self-destruction would be an insult to God. There was also her sensitivity to pain and her fear of it. This woman, who dreaded pain so much, suffered fifteen months of physical agony in her attempt to survive leukemia. Her desire to live, when she knew that her chances were poor, astonished her. Only at one moment during her illness did she seem depressed in the old way (she was not cheerful about leukemia) and it was while her mother lay dying three thousand miles away – the daughter unable to nurse, herself requiring intense care. The hospital psychiatrist in Seattle noted 'suicidal ideation without intent', which may well describe her earlier thoughts and images of self-destruction.

Much of that time, during her last twelve years of physical health, Jane dropped low, she suffered, but she functioned; she wrote poems especially as she climbed out of depression. Her most direct account is 'Having It Out with Melancholy'. It pained her to write this poem. It pained her to expose herself. But writing the poem also helped her to set depression out, as she knew it, depression and its joyful tentative departure. She wanted the poem to help others who were afflicted. The first time she read it aloud, in 1991 at the Frost Place in Franconia, she paused during her reading, resisting tears. When she ended, a line of people waited to talk with her: depressives, people from the families of depressives.

When Jane was mildly depressed, medium-depressed, supported by drugs but weary and fatigued and without serenity, she found a way to raise her spirits and energy for a few hours. In her worst blackness, I could not touch her, but in grayness an orgasm would make her happy and eager to work. She leapt out of bed to write or garden. Therefore, we made love whether we felt like it or not. Endorphins restored, for a moment, energy and the desire to work. Sometimes her climax was merely distant thunder. Such a side effect banished Paxil to the wastebasket.

Mania became obvious first in 1984, but looking back I can recall earlier moments, including a prolonged mystical experience in 1980. She felt the presence of the Holy Ghost, and felt that the spirit was female. The presence passed but its memory remained. Mystics are bipolar: Gerard Manley Hopkins wrote sonnets of ecstasy and sonnets of despair; St John of the Cross described the dark night of the soul. If God enters the human spirit, why should he not use the brain's wiring?

Of her 1984 mania I remember most clearly two or three months, spring and summer of that year. During this first extended elation, I did not know what I confronted. I thought I must learn to live with an entirely changed woman; I am married to someone I don't know. Frugal Jane had to buy a peridot ring; indecisive Jane, who always asked me to make choices – what restaurant to go to, which night to see the play, what book to read aloud – knew *exactly* what we should do, when and where. In her superabundant energy she was bossy: Before, she had hidden in my shadow; now she charged forward as bright as the sun of June. She was consumed by desire; on her thirty-seventh birthday we seemed to make love all day long.

The radical change confused and upset me. When Jane went manic I fell into depression. She soared up and I plunged down – a moody seesaw. I felt 'suicidal ideation without intent'. Then I understood, with shame, that for years I had used her depression to think well of myself: I was the rock, unchanging in all weathers; I was the protector. Now her manic elation and her certainty cast me down. After this first episode of her mania and my response, I put away my complacent self-congratulation.

She fell into depression after mania ceased. Six months later she turned manic again, weeks not months, and spoke carelessly, hurtfully, without malicious intent – in ways she would not have done without mania. By this time I knew what was happening. Thereafter, mania was brief.

Her friends sympathised entirely with her depression but also suffered. Although we were relatively reclusive, we had friends at our church, poet friends who came for weekends, old friends from Ann Arbor, our families. Jane when she was well spent more time in company than I did, lunching with women friends in New London twelve miles away. Her closest friends were two other writers, Alice Mattison and Joyce Peseroff. They saw each other when they could, and workshopped together several times a year. The excitement of their meetings exhausted and elevated Jane. Depression never canceled a workshop, but once she asked Alice not to come calling from a summer place in Vermont. Every month Jane and I drove to Connecticut to see my mother, in her eighties, to shop for her and to visit. Several times, when she was depressed, I had to drive down alone. Sometimes I put visitors off at Jane's urging. I telephoned a dying friend to tell him he could not visit. I canceled a skiing visit from my son and friends because Jane could not see anyone. Every summer Jane's brother, sister-in-law, and niece visited from Ann Arbor. Once I had to telephone and ask them not to come. It was generally I who telephoned, at Jane's request, because she could not herself make the call. On occasion when acquaintances made briefer visits, Jane remained in the bedroom with the door closed while I sat talking with them elsewhere.

One of the hardest things, if you are depressed, is to try to hold yourself up in the presence of others, especially others whom you love. I remember a birthday for granddaughters at my daughter's house. Jane stood looking on, wretched, hardly able to speak. She was quiet, there were many people, and she practiced invisibility. My daughter looked at her and said, 'You're miserable, aren't you?' When Jane nodded Philippa spoke with sympathy and left her alone. You do not try to cheer up depressives; the worst thing you can do is to count their blessings for them.

Depression was a third party in our marriage. There were many happy third parties: poetry, lovemaking, the church, reading Henry James aloud, watching baseball, afternoons spent swimming and sunbathing by Eagle Pond. There were evenings of raucous laughter with friends, not mania but gaiety. Yet depression's ghost was omnipresent for both of us, in dread if not in actuality. She was obdurate in the face of it, trying to be well, writing out of depression to exorcise the illness for her own sake and for the sake of others. Then listlessness and sorrow and self-loathing would overcome her again; then with new medication she would return again to her daily life.

BACK

We try a new drug, a new combination
of drugs, and suddenly
I fall into my life again

like a vole picked up by a storm
then dropped three valleys
and two mountains away from home.

I can find my way back. I know
I will recognise the store
where I used to buy milk and gas.

I remember the house and barn,
the rake, the blue cups and plates,
the Russian novels I loved so much,

and the black silk nightgown
that he once thrust
into the toe of my Christmas stocking.

Jane always understood that her melancholia was inherited, present from birth, but she did not go on medication until after her father's death. Maybe long-term caregivers are more prone to subsequent depression, or to exacerbation of depression – even more prone than people shocked by a sudden unexpected death, who grieve for words unspoken. (With a long illness, everything can be said – if anything can be said.) Trauma affects the chemistry of the brain. The death of the cared-for one – as well as the desperate prolonged caregiving itself, which failed in its purpose – may make changes in the brain like the changes of post-traumatic stress syndrome. For fifteen months I sat by Jane's side, obsessed by her leukemia and her suffering. In the hospital I fetched warm blankets and made lists of questions for our hematologist. At home I saw to her pills, and infused her with food and drink and chemicals. I helped her walk and cleaned up after her.

After she died, I was miserable in my grief. I screamed, I spoke to her pictures and at her grave, I wrote her letters in verse. I dreamed that she had run off with another man; I could not sleep because I dreaded dreaming. But I was not depressed in the way that Jane had been depressed.

It has been observed that the survivor often takes on characteristics of the dead. To embody them? To fill the vacancy? Six months after Jane's death I found myself standing near the birdfeeder with Peterson's *Guide* in my hand. The birds had been Jane's preserve for twenty years at the farm. I thought birds were just fine, I loved their song, but I didn't know one from another. With Jane gone I was taking her place.

Jane was affected by the growing darkness of October, November, December, along with her other symptoms. I had always enjoyed the short days: They felt cozy. Late autumn in the year of her death, something like Seasonal Affective Disorder overcame me. I brought her light box from her study to the top of my desk. Then, thirteen months after her death, I became manic for three months: I lost twenty pounds, slept two or three hours a night, and pursued women boldly. Perhaps my sexual need was a response to nightmares of Jane's adulterous abandonment. Perhaps it was *eros* doing combat with *thanatos*. (I think of how love-making lifted Jane for a moment from gray depression.) Perhaps it was only the familiar symptom of mania. Amazed at my elderly energy, I never considered that I was manic or hypomanic until I crashed into despair and murderous rage, rapidly cycling. (I sought help, and have been helped.) Maybe I perpetuated Jane by imitating her. Maybe inherent bipolarity became activated, the brain altered because of caregiving, failure, and loss.

Jane concluded a poem, begun after her father died, 'Oh, when am I going to own my mind again.'

FURTHER READING

Let Evening Come is a selection introducing Jane Kenyon's work to readers in Britain and Ireland. Other titles by or about her can be ordered via *Amazon.com* (or in some cases from *Amazon.co.uk*), including:

BY JANE KENYON

Otherwise: NEW & SELECTED POEMS (Graywolf Press, 1996)

A Hundred White Daffodils: ESSAYS, INTERVIEWS, THE AKHMATOVA TRANSLATIONS, NEWSPAPER COLUMNS & ONE POEM (Graywolf Press, 1999)

Collected Poems (Graywolf Press, 2005)

ABOUT JANE KENYON

Donald Hall: *The Best Day The Worst Day: Life with Jane Kenyon* (Houghton Mifflin, 2005)

Joyce Peseroff (ed.): *Simply Lasting: Writers on Jane Kenyon* (Graywolf Press, 2005)

from

FROM ROOM TO ROOM

(1978)

For the Night

The mare kicks
in her darkening stall, knocks
over a bucket.
The goose...
The cow keeps a peaceful brain
behind her broad face.
Last light moves
through cracks in the wall,
over bales of hay.
And the bat lets
go of the rafter, falls
into black air.

From Room to Room

Here in this house, among photographs
of your ancestors, their hymnbooks and old
shoes...

        I move from room to room,
a little dazed, like the fly. I watch it
bump against each window.
I am clumsy here, thrusting
slabs of maple into the stove.
Out of my body for a while,
weightless in space....

                Sometimes
the wind against the clapboard
sounds like a car driving up to the house.

My people are not here, my mother
and father, my brother. I talk
to the cats about weather.

'Blessed be the tie that binds...'
we sing in the church down the road.
And how does it go from there? The tie...

the tether, the hose carrying
oxygen to the astronaut,
turning, turning outside the hatch,
taking a look around.

Here

You always belonged here.
You were theirs, certain as a rock.
I'm the one who worries
if I fit in with the furniture
and the landscape.

But I 'follow too much
the devices and desires of my own heart'.

Already the curves in the road
are familiar to me, and the mountain
in all kinds of light,
treating all people the same.
And when I come over the hill,
I see the house, with its generous
and firm proportions, smoke
rising gaily from the chimney.

I feel my life start up again,
like a cutting when it grows
the first pale and tentative
root hair in a glass of water.

Two Days Alone

You are not here. I keep
the fire going, though it isn't cold,
feeding the stove-animal.
I read the evening paper
with five generations
looking over my shoulder.

In the woodshed
darkness is all around and inside me.
The only sound I hear
is my own breathing. Maybe
I don't belong here.
Nothing tells me that I don't.

Finding a Long Gray Hair

I scrub the long floorboards
in the kitchen, repeating
the motions of other women
who have lived in this house.
And when I find a long gray hair
floating in the pail,
I feel my life added to theirs.

The Needle

Grandmother, you are as pale
as Christ's hands on the wall above you.
When you close your eyes you are all
white – hair, skin, gown. I blink
to find you again in the bed.

I remember once you told me
you weighed a hundred and twenty-three,
the day you married Grandfather.
You had handsome legs. He watched you
working at the sink.

The soft ring is loose on your hand.
I hated coming here.
I know you can't understand me.
I'll try again,
like the young nurse with the needle.

The Shirt

The shirt touches his neck
and smooths over his back.
It slides down his sides.
It even goes down below his belt –
down into his pants.
Lucky shirt.

Falling

March. Rain. Five days now.
Water gathers in flat places,
finds every space between stones.
The river peaks, fish lie
stunned on the muddy bottom.

After the crash in the Swiss
countryside, an arm
dangles from a tree. A tortoiseshell
comb parts the grass.
The bookmark is still in place.

This month I was five days late,
but now the blood comes in a rush.
Let everything fall where it will.
Someone unpacks a suitcase, thinks
of living without possessions.

Afternoon in the House

It's quiet here. The cats
sprawl, each
in a favored place.
The geranium leans this way
to see if I'm writing about her:
head all petals, brown
stalks, and those green fans.
So you see,
I am writing about you.

I turn on the radio. Wrong.
Let's not have any noise
in this room, except
the sound of a voice reading a poem.
The cats request
The Meadow Mouse, by Theodore Roethke.

The house settles down on its haunches
for a doze.
I know you are with me, plants,
and cats – and even so, I'm frightened,
sitting in the middle of perfect
possibility.

Full Moon in Winter

Bare branches rise
and fall overhead.
The barn door bangs loose,
persistent as remorse
after anger and shouting.
Dogs bark across the pond.
The shadow of the house
appears on the crusted snow
like the idea of a house,
and my own shadow
lies down in the cold
at my feet, lunatic,
like someone tired
of living in a body,
needy and full of desire....

Year Day

We are living together on the earth.
The clock's heart
beats in its wooden chest.
The cats follow the sun through the house.
We lie down together at night.

Today, you work in your office,
and I in my study. Sometimes
we are busy and casual.
Sitting here, I can see
the path we have made on the rug.

The hermit gives up
after thirty years of hiding in the jungle.
The last door to the last room
comes unlatched. Here are the gestures
of my hands. Wear them in your hair.

The Suitor

We lie back to back. Curtains
lift and fall,
like the chest of someone sleeping.
Wind moves the leaves of the box elder;
they show their light undersides,
turning all at once
like a school of fish.
Suddenly I understand that I am happy.
For months this feeling
has been coming closer, stopping
for short visits, like a timid suitor.

from

THE BOAT OF QUIET HOURS

(1986)

Evening at a Country Inn

From here I see a single red cloud
impaled on the Town Hall weather vane.
Now the horses are back in their stalls,
and the dogs are nowhere in sight
that made them run and buck
in the brittle morning light.

You laughed only once all day –
when the cat ate cucumbers
in Chekhov's story...and now you smoke
and pace the long hallway downstairs.

The cook is roasting meat for the evening meal,
and the smell rises to all the rooms.
Red-faced skiers stamp past you
on their way in; their hunger is Homeric.

I know you are thinking of the accident –
of picking the slivered glass from his hair.
Just now a truck loaded with hay
stopped at the village store to get gas.
I wish you would look at the hay –
the beautiful sane and solid bales of hay.

Back from the City

After three days and nights of rich food
and late talk in overheated rooms,
of walks between mounds of garbage
and human forms bedded down for the night
under rags, I come back to my dooryard,
to my own wooden step.

The last red leaves fall to the ground
and frost has blackened the herbs and asters
that grew beside the porch. The air
is still and cool, and the withered grass
lies flat in the field. A nuthatch spirals
down the rough trunk of the tree.

At the Cloisters I indulged in piety
while gazing at a painted lindenwood Pietà –
Mary holding her pierced and desiccated son
across her knees; but when a man stepped close
under the tasseled awning of the hotel,
asking for 'a quarter for someone
down on his luck', I quickly turned my back.

Now I hear tiny bits of bark and moss
break off under the bird's beak and claw,
and fall onto already-fallen leaves.
'Do you love me?' said Christ to his disciple.
'Lord, you know
that I love you.'
                           'Then feed my sheep.'

47

November Calf

She calved in the ravine, beside
the green-scummed pond.
Full clouds and mist hung low –
it was unseasonably warm. Steam
rose from her head as she pushed
and called; her cries went out
over the still-lush fields.

First came the front feet, then
the blossom-nose, shell-pink
and glistening; and then the broad
forehead, flopping black ears,
and neck.... She worked
until the steaming length of him
rushed out onto the ground, then
turned and licked him with her wide
pink tongue. He lifted up his head
and looked around.

The herd pressed close to see, then
frolicked up the bank, flicking
their tails. It looked like revelry.
The farmer set off for the barn,
swinging in a widening arc
a frayed and knotted scrap of rope.

Rain in January

I woke before dawn, still
in a body. Water ran
down every window, and rushed
from the eaves.

Beneath the empty feeder
a skunk was prowling for suet
or seed. The lamps flickered off
and then came on again.

Smoke from the chimney
could not rise. It came down
into the yard, and brooded there
on the unlikelihood of reaching

heaven. When my arm slipped
from the arm of the chair
I let it hang beside me, pale,
useless, and strange.

Depression in Winter

There comes a little space between the south
side of a boulder
and the snow that fills the woods around it.
Sun heats the stone, reveals
a crescent of bare ground: brown ferns,
and tufts of needles like red hair,
acorns, a patch of moss, bright green....

I sank with every step up to my knees,
throwing myself forward with a violence
of effort, greedy for unhappiness –
until by accident I found the stone,
with its secret porch of heat and light,
where something small could luxuriate, then
turned back down my path, chastened and calm.

Ice Storm

For the hemlocks and broad-leafed evergreens
a beautiful and precarious state of being....
Here in the suburbs of New Haven
nature, unrestrained, lops the weaker limbs
of shrubs and trees with a sense of aesthetics
that is practical and sinister....

I am a guest in this house.
On the bedside table *Good Housekeeping*, and
A Nietzsche Reader.... The others are still asleep.
The most painful longing comes over me.
A longing not of the body....

It could be for beauty –
I mean what Keats was panting after,
for which I love and honor him;
it could be for the promises of God;
or for oblivion, *nada*; or some condition even more
extreme, which I intuit, but can't quite name.

Walking Alone in Late Winter

How long the winter has lasted – like a Mahler
symphony, or an hour in the dentist's chair.
In the fields the grasses are matted
and gray, making me think of June, when hay
and vetch burgeon in the heat, and warm rain
swells the globed buds of the peony.

Ice on the pond breaks into huge planes. One
sticks like a barge gone awry at the neck
of the bridge.... The reeds
and shrubby brush along the shore
gleam with ice that shatters when the breeze
moves them. From beyond the bog
the sound of water rushing over trees
felled by the zealous beavers,
who bring them crashing down.... Sometimes
it seems they do it just for fun.

Those days of anger and remorse
come back to me; you fidgeting with your ring,
sliding it off, then jabbing it on again.

The wind is keen coming over the ice;
it carries the sound of breaking glass.
And the sun, bright but not warm,
has gone behind the hill. Chill, or the fear
of chill, sends me hurrying home.

The Pond at Dusk

A fly wounds the water but the wound
soon heals. Swallows tilt and twitter
overhead, dropping now and then toward
the outward-radiating evidence of food.

The green haze on the trees changes
into leaves, and what looks like smoke
floating over the neighbor's barn
is only apple blossoms.

But sometimes what looks like disaster
is disaster: the day comes at last,
and the men struggle with the casket
just clearing the pews.

High Water

Eight days of rain;
the ground refuses more.
My neighbors are morose at the village store.

I'm sick of holding still, sick of indoors,
so I walk through the heavy-headed grasses
to watch the river reach
for the bridge's wooden planks,
bending the lithe swamp maples
that grow along the banks.

Nothing but trouble comes to mind
as I lean over the rusty iron rail.
I know of plenty, in detail, that is not
my own. I nudge a pebble over the edge.
It drops with a *thunk* into the water –
dark, voluminous, and clear,
and moving headlong away from here.

Evening Sun

Why does this light force me back
to my childhood? I wore a yellow
summer dress, and the skirt
made a perfect circle.

                        Turning and turning
until it flared to the limit
was irresistible.... The grass and trees,
my outstretched arms, and the skirt
whirled in the ochre light
of an early June evening.

                        And I knew then
that I would have to live, and go on
living: what a sorrow it was; and still
what sorrow burns
but does not destroy my heart.

Summer 1890: Near the Gulf

The hour was late, and the others
were asleep. He struck a match
on the wooden railing of the porch
and lit a cigarette

while she beheld his head and hand,
estranged from the body
in wavering light....

What she felt then
would, like heavy wind
and rain, bring
any open flower to the ground.

He let the spent match
fall; but the face remained
before her, like a bright light
before a closed eye....

The Sandy Hole

The infant's coffin no bigger than a flightbag....
The young father steps backward from the sandy hole,
eyes wide and dry, his hand over his mouth.
No one dares to come near him, even to touch his sleeve.

February: Thinking of Flowers

Now wind torments the field,
turning the white surface back
on itself, back and back on itself,
like an animal licking a wound.

Nothing but white – the air, the light;
only one brown milkweed pod
bobbing in the gully, smallest
brown boat on the immense tide.

A single green sprouting thing
would restore me....

Then think of the tall delphinium,
swaying, or the bee when it comes
to the tongue of the burgundy lily.

Portrait of a Figure Near Water

Rebuked, she turned and ran
uphill to the barn. Anger, the inner
arsonist, held a match to her brain.
She observed her life: against her will
it survived the unwavering flame.

The barn was empty of animals.
Only a swallow tilted
near the beams, and bats
hung from the rafters
the roof sagged between.

Her breath became steady
where, years past, the farmer cooled
the big tin amphorae of milk.
The stone trough was still
filled with water: she watched it
and received its calm.

So it is when we retreat in anger:
we think we burn alone
and there is no balm.
Then water enters, though it makes
no sound.

Thinking of Madame Bovary

The first hot April day the granite step
was warm. Flies droned in the grass.
When a car went past they rose
in unison, then dropped back down....

I saw that a yellow crocus bud had pierced
a dead oak leaf, then opened wide. How strong
its appetite for the luxury of the sun!

Everyone longs for love's tense joys and red delights.

And then I spied an ant
dragging a ragged, disembodied wing
up the warm brick walk. It must have been
the Methodist in me that leaned forward,
preceded by my shadow, to put a twig just where
the ant was struggling with its own desire.

Philosophy in Warm Weather

Now all the doors and windows
are open, and we move so easily
through the rooms. Cats roll
on the sunny rugs, and a clumsy wasp
climbs the pane, pausing
to rub a leg over her head.

All around physical life reconvenes.
The molecules of our bodies must love
to exist: they whirl in circles
and seem to begrudge us nothing.
Heat, Horatio, *heat* makes them
put this antic disposition on!

This year's brown spider
sways over the door as I come
and go. A single poppy shouts
from the far field, and the crow,
beyond alarm, goes right on
pulling up the corn.

The Bat

I was reading about rationalism,
the kind of thing we do up north
in early winter, where the sun
leaves work for the day at 4:15.
Maybe the world is intelligible
to the rational mind;
and maybe we light the lamps at dusk
for nothing....

Then I heard wings overhead.

The cats and I chased the bat
in circles – living room, kitchen,
pantry, kitchen, living room....
At every turn it evaded us

like the identity of the third person
in the Trinity: the one
who spoke through the prophets,
the one who astounded Mary
by suddenly coming near.

Trouble with Math in a One-Room Country School

The others bent their heads and started in.
Confused, I asked my neighbor
to explain – a sturdy, bright-cheeked girl
who brought raw milk to school from her family's
herd of Holsteins. Ann had a blue bookmark,
and on it Christ revealed his beating heart,
holding the flesh back with His wounded hand.
Ann understood division....

Miss Moran sprang from her monumental desk
and led me roughly through the class
without a word. My shame was radical
as she propelled me past the cloakroom
to the furnace closet, where only the boys
were put, only the older ones at that.
The door swung briskly shut.

The warmth, the gloom, the smell
of sweeping compound clinging to the broom
soothed me. I found a bucket, turned it
upside down, and sat, hugging my knees.
I hummed a theme from Haydn that I knew
from my piano lessons...
and hardened my heart against authority.
And then I heard her steps, her fingers
on the latch. She led me, blinking
and changed, back to the class.

The Little Boat

As soon as spring peepers sounded from the stream
and boggy lower barnyard across the road
Mother let us bring out the cots,
and sleeping bags – red and gray and black
plaid flannel, still smelling of the cedar chest.

How hard it was to settle down that first night
out on the big screened porch: three times
trains passed the crossing, and the peepers' song
was lost under the whistle (two long,
two short), the rumble and clacking,
and clang of the crossing bell. The neighbor's
cocker spaniel howled the whole time
and for a full two minutes after.... Or rain
sluiced from the eaves, and we saw black limbs
against a sky whitened by lightning.
The gloom was lavish and agreeable....

August came. Mother took us to Wahr's on State Street,
bought each of us a reader, speller, Big 10 Tablet,
a bottle of amber glue with a slit like a closed eye,
pencils, erasers of a violent pink, a penmanship workbook
for practicing loops that looked to me
like the culvert under the road, whose dark and webby length
Brother and I dared each other to run through...
and crayons, the colors ranging from one to another
until what began as yellow ended amazingly as blue.

One morning we walked to the top of Foster Road,
and stood under the Reimers' big maple.
Ground fog rose from the hay stubble.
We heard gears grinding at the foot of the hill;
the bus appeared and we knew we had to get in.
All day in my imagination my body floated
above the classroom, navigating easily

between fluorescent shoals.... I was listening,
floating, watching.... The others stayed below
at their desks (I saw the crown of my own head
bending over a book), and no one knew I was not
where I seemed to be....

Song

An oriole sings from the hedge
and in the hotel kitchen
the chef sweetens cream for pastries.
Far off, lightning and thunder agree
to join us for a few days
here in the valley. How lucky we are
to be holding hands on a porch
in the country. But even this
is not the joy that trembles
under every leaf and tongue.

Coming Home at Twilight in Late Summer

We turned into the drive,
and gravel flew up from the tires
like sparks from a fire. So much
to be done – the unpacking, the mail
and papers... the grass needed mowing....
We climbed stiffly out of the car.
The shut-off engine ticked as it cooled.

And then we noticed the pear tree,
the limbs so heavy with fruit
they nearly touched the ground.
We went out to the meadow; our steps
made black holes in the grass;
and we each took a pear,
and ate, and were grateful.

After Traveling

While in silence I rake
my plot of grass under the great trees –
the oaks and monumental maples –
I think of the proprietor

of the Caffè dei Fiori, sleepy, preoccupied,
dressed to the nines,
setting out tables in the Via Frattina –
extending his empire each day
by the smallest of increments
until there is room for another place...

at which we happen to be sitting
on the day the city official comes,
also dressed to the nines, to unwind
his shining metal measure in the street:
two tables must go. But for now
the proprietor shrugs, and a look
of infinite weariness passes
over his face. This is Rome:
remorse would be anomalous....

And the white-coated waiters
arrange on doilied silver trays
the tiers of sugared pastries: angel wings,
cat tongues, and little kiwi tarts;
and the coffee machines fizzle and spurt
such appetising steam; and a woman
in a long red cape goes by
leading a matched pair of pugs
on a bifurcated leash.

Twilight: After Haying

Yes, long shadows go out
from the bales; and yes, the soul
must part from the body:
what else could it do?

The men sprawl near the baler,
too tired to leave the field.
They talk and smoke,
and the tips of their cigarettes
blaze like small roses
in the night air. (It arrived
and settled among them
before they were aware.)

The moon comes
to count the bales,
and the dispossessed –
Whip-poor-will, Whip-poor-will
– sings from the dusty stubble.

These things happen... the soul's bliss
and suffering are bound together
like the grasses....
The last, sweet exhalations
of timothy and vetch
go out with the song of the bird;
the ravaged field
grows wet with dew.

Who

These lines are written
by an animal, an angel,
a stranger sitting in my chair;
by someone who already knows
how to live without trouble
among books, and pots and pans....

Who is it who asks me to find
language for the sound
a sheep's hoof makes when it strikes
a stone? And who speaks
the words which are my food?

Briefly It Enters, and Briefly Speaks

I am the blossom pressed in a book,
found again after two hundred years....

I am the maker, the lover, and the keeper....

When the young girl who starves
sits down to a table
she will sit beside me....

I am food on the prisoner's plate....

I am water rushing to the wellhead,
filling the pitcher until it spills....

I am the patient gardener
of the dry and weedy garden....

I am the stone step,
the latch, and the working hinge....

I am the heart contracted by joy...
the longest hair, white
before the rest....

I am there in the basket of fruit
presented to the widow....

I am the musk rose opening
unattended, the fern on the boggy summit....

I am the one whose love
overcomes you, already with you
when you think to call my name....

Things

The hen flings a single pebble aside
with her yellow, reptilian foot.
Never in eternity the same sound –
a small stone falling on a red leaf.

The juncture of twig and branch,
scarred with lichen, is a gate
we might enter, singing.

The mouse pulls batting
from a hundred-year-old quilt.
She chewed a hole in a blue star
to get it, and now she thrives....
Now is her time to thrive.

Things: simply lasting, then
failing to last: water, a blue heron's
eye, and the light passing
between them: into light all things
must fall, glad at last to have fallen.

from

LET EVENING COME

(1990)

Three Songs at the End of Summer

A second crop of hay lies cut
and turned. Five gleaming crows
search and peck between the rows.
They make a low, companionable squawk,
and like midwives and undertakers
possess a weird authority.

Crickets leap from the stubble,
parting before me like the Red Sea.
The garden sprawls and spoils.

Across the lake the campers have learned
to water-ski. They have, or they haven't.
Sounds of the instructor's megaphone
suffuse the hazy air. 'Relax! Relax!'

Cloud shadows rush over drying hay,
fences, dusty lane, and railroad ravine.
The first yellowing fronds of goldenrod
brighten the margins of the woods.

Schoolbooks, carpools, pleated skirts;
water, silver-still, and a vee of geese.

*

The cicada's dry monotony breaks
over me. The days are bright
and free, bright and free.

Then why did I cry today
for an hour, with my whole
body, the way babies cry?

*

A white, indifferent morning sky,
and a crow, hectoring from its nest
high in the hemlock, a nest as big
as a laundry basket....
                              In my childhood
I stood under a dripping oak,
while autumnal fog eddied around my feet,
waiting for the school bus
with a dread that took my breath away.

The damp dirt road gave off
this same complex organic scent.

I had the new books – words, numbers,
and operations with numbers I did not
comprehend – and crayons, unspoiled
by use, in a blue canvas satchel
with red leather straps.

Spruce, inadequate, and alien
I stood at the side of the road.
It was the only life I had.

Catching Frogs

I crouched beside the deepest pool,
and the smell of damp and moss
rose rich between my knees. Water-striders
creased the silver-black silky surface.
Rapt, I hardly breathed. Gnats
roiled in a shaft of sun.

Back again after supper I'd see
a nose poke up by the big flat stone
at the lip of the fall; then the humped
eyes and the slippery emerald head,
freckled brown. The buff membrane
pulsed under the jaw while
subtleties of timing played in my mind.

With a patience that came like grace
I waited. Mosquitoes moaned all
around. Better to wait. Better to reach
from behind.... It grew dark.

I came into the warm, bright room
where Father held aloft the evening
paper, and there was talk, and maybe
laughter, though I don't remember laughter.

In the Grove: The Poet at Ten

She lay on her back in the timothy
and gazed past the doddering
auburn heads of sumac.

A cloud – huge, calm,
and dignified – covered the sun
but did not, could not, put it out.

The light surged back again.

Nothing could rouse her then
from that joy so violent
it was hard to distinguish from pain.

The Pear

There is a moment in middle age
when you grow bored, angered
by your middling mind,
afraid.

That day the sun
burns hot and bright,
making you more desolate.

It happens subtly, as when a pear
spoils from the inside out,
and you may not be aware
until things have gone too far.

After the Dinner Party

A late-blooming burgundy hollyhock sways
across the kitchen window in a light breeze
as I draw a tumbler of well-water at the sink.
We're face to face, as in St Paul's Epistles
or the later novels of Henry James.

The cold rains of autumn have begun.
Driving to Hanover I must have seen
a thousand frogs in the headlights
crossing the gleaming road. Like sheep urged
by a crouching dog they converged
and flowed, as they do every fall.
I couldn't help hitting some.

At dinner I laughed with the rest,
but in truth I prefer the sound
of pages turning, and coals shifting
abruptly in the stove. I left before ten
pleading a long drive home.

The smell of woodsmoke hung
over the small villages along the way.

I passed the huge cold gray stone
buildings left by the chaste Shakers.
Any window will still open with one finger.
Hands to work, and hearts to God....

Why do people give dinner parties? Why did I
say I'd come? I suppose no one there was entirely
at ease. Again the flower leans this way:
you know it's impolite to stare. I'll put
out the light.... And there's an end to it.

The Letter

Bad news arrives in her distinctive hand.
The cancer has returned, this time
to his brain. Surgery impossible,
treatments underway. Hair loss, bouts
of sleeplessness and agitation at night,
exhaustion during the day....

I snap the blue leash onto the D-ring
of the dog's collar, and we cross
Route 4, then cut through the hayfield
to the pond road, where I let him run
along with my morbidity.

The trees have leafed out – only just –
and the air is misty with sap.
So green, so brightly, richly succulent,
this arbor over the road....
Sunlight penetrates in golden drops.

We come to the place where a neighbor
is taking timber from his land.
There's a smell of lacerated earth
and pine. Hardwood smells different.
His truck is gone.

Now you can see well up the slope,
see ledges of rock and ferns breaking forth
among the stumps and cast-aside limbs
and branches.

The place will heal itself in time, first
with weeds – goldenrod, cinquefoil, moth
mullein, then blackberries, sapling
pine, deciduous trees... but for now

the dog rolls, jovial, in the pungent
disturbance of wood and earth.

I summon him with a word, turn back,
and we go the long way home.

We Let the Boat Drift

I set out for the pond, crossing the ravine
where seedling pines start up like sparks
between the disused rails of the Boston and Maine.

The grass in the field would make a second crop
if early autumn rains hadn't washed
the goodness out. After the night's hard frost
it makes a brittle rustling as I walk.

The water is utterly still. Here and there
a black twig sticks up. It's five years today,
and even now I can't accept what cancer did
to him – not death so much as the annihilation
of the whole man, sense by sense, thought
by thought, hope by hope.

Once we talked about the life to come.
I took the Bible from the nightstand
and offered John 14: 'I go to prepare
a place for you.' 'Fine. Good,' he said.
'But what about Matthew? "You, therefore,
must be perfect, as your heavenly Father
is perfect."' And he wept.

My neighbor honks and waves driving by.
She counsels troubled students; keeps bees;
her goats follow her to the mailbox.

Last Sunday afternoon we went canoeing on the pond.
Something terrible at school had shaken her.
We talked quietly far from shore. The paddles
rested across our laps; glittering drops
fell randomly from their tips. The light
around us seemed alive. A loon – itinerant –
let us get quite close before it dove, coming up
after a long time, and well away from humankind.

Spring Changes

The autumnal drone of my neighbor
cutting wood across the pond
and the soundlessness of winter
give way to hammering. Must be
he's roofing, or building a shed
or fence. Some form of spring-induced
material advance.

Mother called early to say she's sold the house.
I'll fly out, help her sort and pack,
and give and throw away. One thing I'd like:
the yellow hand-painted pottery
vase that's crimped at the edge
like the crust of a pie – so gay, but
they almost never used it, who knows why?

A new young pair will paint and mow,
and fix the picket fence, wash windows face
to face in May, he outside on a ladder,
she inside on a chair, mouthing kisses
and 'Be Careful!' through the glass.

April Chores

When I take the chilly tools
from the shed's darkness, I come
out to a world made new
by heat and light.

The snake basks and dozes
on a large flat stone.
It reared and scolded me
for raking too close to its hole.

Like a mad red brain
the involute rhubarb leaf
thinks its way up
through loam.

The Clearing

The dog and I push through the ring
of dripping junipers
to enter the open space high on the hill
where I let him off the leash.

He vaults, snuffling, between tufts of moss;
twigs snap beneath his weight; he rolls
and rubs his jowls on the aromatic earth;
his pink tongue lolls.

I look for sticks of proper heft
to throw for him, while he sits, prim
and earnest in his love, if it is love.

All night a soaking rain, and now the hill
exhales relief, and the fragrance
of warm earth…. The sedges
have grown an inch since yesterday,
and ferns unfurled, and even if they try
the lilacs by the barn can't
keep from opening today.

I longed for spring's thousand tender greens,
and the white-throated sparrow's call
that borders on rudeness. Do you know –
since you went away
all I can do
is wait for you to come back to me.

Work

It has been light since four. In June
the birds find plenty to remark upon
at that hour. Pickup trucks, three men
to a cab, rush past burgeoning hay
and corn to summer constructions
up in town.
        Here, soon, the mowing, raking
and baling will begin. And I must tell
how, before the funeral all those years ago,
we lay down briefly on your grandparents'
bed, and that when you stood to put on
your jacket the change slipped
from your pants pocket.

Some dropped on the chenille
spread, and some hit the threadbare rug,
and one coin rolled onto the wide pine
floorboard under the dresser, hit
the molding, teetered and fell silent
like the rest. And oh, your sigh –
the sigh you sighed then....

At the Spanish Steps in Rome

Keats had come with his friend Severn
for the mild Roman winter. Afternoons
they walked to the Borghese Gardens
to see fine ladies, nannies with babies,
and handsome mounted officers,
whose horses moved sedately
along the broad and sandy paths.

But soon the illness kept him in.
Severn kept trying in that stoutly
cheerful English way: he rented a spinet,
hauled it three flights, turning it end
up on the landings, and played Haydn every day.

Love letters lay unopened in a chest.
'To see her hand writing would break my heart.'

The poet's anger rose as his health sank.
He began to refer to his 'posthumous
existence'. One day while Severn and the porter
watched he flung, dish by dish, his catered
meal into the street.

Now the room where Keats died is a museum,
closed for several hours midday with the rest
of Rome. Waiting on the Steps in the wan
October sun I see the curator's pale,
exceptionally round face looking down.
Everything that was not burned that day
in accordance with the law is there.

Staying at Grandma's

Sometimes they left me for the day
while they went – what does it matter
where – away. I sat and watched her work
the dough, then turn the white shape
yellow in a buttered bowl.

A coleus, wrong to my eye because its leaves
were red, was rooting on the sill
in a glass filled with water and azure
marbles. I loved to see the sun
pass through the blue.

'You know,' she'd say, turning
her straight and handsome back to me,
'that the body is the temple
of the Holy Ghost.'

The Holy Ghost, the oh, oh…the *uh*
oh, I thought, studying the toe of my new shoe,
and glad she wasn't looking at me.

Soon I'd be back in school. No more mornings
at Grandma's side while she swept the walk
or shook the dust mop by the neck.

If she loved me why did she say that
two women would be grinding at the mill,
that God would come out of the clouds
when they were least expecting him,
choose one to be with him in heaven
and leave the other there alone?

A Boy Goes into the World

My brother rode off on his bike
into the summer afternoon, but
Mother called me back
from the end of the sandy drive:
'It's different for girls.'

He'd be gone for hours, come back
with things: a cocoon, gray-brown
and papery around a stick;
a puff ball, ripe, wrinkled,
and exuding spores; owl pellets –
bits of undigested bone and fur;
and pieces of moss that might
have made toupees for preposterous
green men, but went instead
into a wide-necked jar for a terrarium.

He mounted his plunder on poster
board, gluing and naming
each piece. He has long since
forgotten those days and things, but
I at last can claim them as my own.

Lines for Akhmatova

The night train from Moscow, beginning to slow,
pulled closer to your sleeping city.
A sound like tiny bells in cold air.... Then
the attendant appeared with glasses of strong tea.
'Wake up, ladies! This is Leningrad.'

The narrow canals gleam black and still
under ornate street lamps, and in the parks
golden leaves lie on the sandy paths
and wooden benches. By light of day
old women dressed in black sweep them away
with birch stick brooms.

Your work, your amorous life, your scholarship –
everything happened here, where the Party
silenced you for twenty-five years
for writing about love – a middle-class activity.

Husband and son, lovers, dear companions
were imprisoned or killed, emigrated or died.
You turned still further inward,
imperturbable as a lion-gate, and lived on
stubbornly, learning Dante by heart.

In the end you outlived the genocidal
Georgian with his mustache thick as a snake.
And in triumph, an old woman, you wrote:
I can't tell if the day is ending, or the world,
or if the secret of secrets is within me again.

September Garden Party

We sit with friends at the round
glass table. The talk is clever;
everyone rises to it. Bees
come to the spiral pear peelings
on your plate.
From my lap or your hand
the spice of our morning's privacy
comes drifting up. Fall sun
passes through the wine.

On the Aisle

Leaving Maui – orchids on our plates,
whales seen from the balcony at cocktail hour,
and Mai Tais bristling with fruit –
we climb through thirty-two thousand feet
with retired schoolteachers, widows on tours,
and honeymooners. The man and woman next to me,
young, large, bronze, and prosperous,
look long without fear or shame
into each other's faces.

Anxious, I am grateful for rum, my last
island draught, and the circulation
of the blood, and I begin Gogol's story
about a painter whose love of luxury
destroys his art. People pull down
their window shades, shutting out the sun,
and a movie called *Clue* comes on.
I continue to read in my pillar of light
like a village schoolmistress, while
from the dark on my right comes
the sound of kissing. It would be a lie
to say I didn't sneak a look.

On the slow approach to rainy San Francisco
I find I had things figured wrong:
'Don't worry, OK? He's still out of town.'
I stop speculating about their occupations
and combined income. They fall silent again.

We hit the runway and bounce three times.
After what seems too long the nose comes down;
I feel the brakes go on. Their grief is real
when my seatmates part at the gate. He has
a close connection to Tucson,
and runs for it.

Father and Son

August. My neighbor started cutting wood
on cool Sabbath afternoons, the blue
plume of the saw's exhaust wavering over
his head. At first I didn't mind the noise
but it came to seem like a species of pain.

From time to time he let the saw idle,
stepping back from the logs and aromatic
dust, while his son kicked the billets
down the sloping drive toward the shed.
In the lull they sometimes talked.

His back ached unrelentingly, he assumed
from all the stooping. Sundays that fall
they bent over the pile of beech and maple,
intent on getting wood for winter, the last,
as it happened, of their life together.

Ice Out

As late as yesterday ice preoccupied
the pond – dark, half-melted, waterlogged.
Then it sank in the night, one piece,
taking winter with it. And afterward
everything seems simple and good.

All afternoon I lifted oak leaves
from the flowerbeds, and greeted
like friends the green-white crowns
of perennials. They have the tender,
unnerving beauty of a baby's head.

How I hated to come in! I've left
the windows open to hear the peepers'
wildly disproportionate cries.
Dinner is over, no one stirs. The dog
sighs, sneezes, and closes his eyes.

Now Where?

It wakes when I wake, walks
when I walk, turns back when I
turn back, beating me to the door.

It spoils my food and steals
my sleep, and mocks me, saying,
'Where is your God now?'

And so, like a widow, I lie down
after supper. If I lie down
or sit up it's all the same:

the days and nights bear me along.
To strangers I must seem
alive. Spring comes, summer;

cool clear weather; heat, rain....

Summer: 6:00 A.M.

From the shadowy upstairs bedroom
of my mother-in-law's house in Hamden
I hear the neighbors' children waking.

'Ahhhhhhhh,' says the infant, not
unhappily. 'Yes, yes, yes, yes, yes!'
replies the toddler to his mother,
who must have forbidden something.
It is hot already at this hour
and the houses are wholly open.
If she is cross with the child
anyone with ears will hear.

The slap of sprinkler water
hitting the sidewalk and street,
and the husband's deliberate footfalls
receding down the drive....

His Japanese sedan matches the house.
Beige, brown... Yesterday he washed it,
his arm thrust deep into something
that looked like a sheepskin oven mitt.

His wife had put the babies
in the shallow plastic wading
pool, and she took snapshots, trying
repeatedly to get both boys to look.
The older one's wail rose
and matched the pitch of the cicada
in a nearby tree. Why
is the sound of a spoon on a plate
next door a thing so desolate?
I think of the woman pouring a glass of juice
for the three-year-old, and watching him
spill it, knowing he *must* spill it,

97

seeing the ineluctable downward course
of the orange-pink liquid, the puddle
swell on the kitchen
floor beside the child's shoe.

Let Evening Come

Let the light of late afternoon
shine through chinks in the barn, moving
up the bales as the sun moves down.

Let the cricket take up chafing
as a woman takes up her needles
and her yarn. Let evening come.

Let dew collect on the hoe abandoned
in long grass. Let the stars appear
and the moon disclose her silver horn.

Let the fox go back to its sandy den.
Let the wind die down. Let the shed
go black inside. Let evening come.

To the bottle in the ditch, to the scoop
in the oats, to air in the lung
let evening come.

Let it come, as it will, and don't
be afraid. God does not leave us
comfortless, so let evening come.

With the Dog at Sunrise

Although we always come this way
I never noticed before that the poplars
growing along the ravine
shine pink in the light of winter dawn.

What am I going to say
in my letter to Sarah – a widow
at thirty-one, alone in the violence
of her grief, sleepless,
and utterly cast down?

I look at the lithe, pink trees more carefully,
remembering Stephen, the photographer.
With the hunger of two I take them in.
Perhaps I can tell her that.

The dog furrows his brow while pissing long
and thoughtfully against an ancient hemlock.
The snow turns the saffron of a monk's robe
and acrid steam ascends.

Searching for God is the first thing and the last,
but in between such trouble, and such pain.

Far up in the woods where no one goes
deer take their ease under the great
pines, nose to steaming nose....

from

CONSTANCE

(1993)

FROM PSALM 139
'O Lord, thou hast searched me...'

Whither shall I go from thy spirit?
    or whither shall I flee from thy presence?
If I ascend up into heaven, thou art there:
    if I make my bed in hell, behold, thou art there.
If I take the wings of the morning,
    and dwell in the uttermost parts of the sea;
Even there shall thy hand lead me,
    and thy right hand shall hold me.
If I say, Surely the darkness shall cover me;
    even the night shall be light about me.
Yea, the darkness hideth not from thee;
    but the night shineth as the day:
    the darkness and the light are both alike in thee...

August Rain, After Haying

Through sere trees and beheaded
grasses the slow rain falls.
Hay fills the barn; only the rake
and one empty wagon are left
in the field. In the ditches
goldenrod bends to the ground.

Even at noon the house is dark.
In my room under the eaves
I hear the steady benevolence
of water washing dust
raised by the haying
from porch and car and garden
chair. We are shorn
and purified, as if tonsured.

The grass resolves to grow again,
receiving the rain to that end,
but my disordered soul thirsts
after something it cannot name.

Biscuit

The dog has cleaned his bowl
and his reward is a biscuit,
which I put in his mouth
like a priest offering the host.

I can't bear that trusting face!
He asks for bread, expects
bread, and I in my power
might have given him a stone.

Not Writing

A wasp rises to its papery
nest under the eaves
where it daubs

at the gray shape,
but seems unable
to enter its own house.

Having It Out with Melancholy

If many remedies are prescribed for an illness,
you may be certain that the illness has no cure.

A.P. CHEKHOV

The Cherry Orchard

1 *From the Nursery*

When I was born, you waited
behind a pile of linen in the nursery,
and when we were alone, you lay down
on top of me, pressing
the bile of desolation into every pore.
And from that day on
everything under the sun and moon
made me sad – even the yellow
wooden beads that slid and spun
along a spindle on my crib.

You taught me to exist without gratitude.
You ruined my manners toward God:
'We're here simply to wait for death;
the pleasures of earth are overrated.'

I only appeared to belong to my mother,
to live among blocks and cotton undershirts
with snaps; among red tin lunch boxes
and report cards in ugly brown slipcases.
I was already yours – the anti-urge,
the mutilator of souls.

2 *Bottles*

Elavil, Ludiomil, Doxepin,
Norpramin, Prozac, Lithium, Xanax,
Wellbutrin, Parnate, Nardil, Zoloft.

The coated ones smell sweet or have
no smell; the powdery ones smell
like the chemistry lab at school
that made me hold my breath.

3 *Suggestion from a Friend*

You wouldn't be so depressed
if you really believed in God.

4 *Often*

Often I go to bed as soon after dinner
as seems adult
(I mean I try to wait for dark)
in order to push away
from the massive pain in sleep's
frail wicker coracle.

5 *Once There Was Light*

Once, in my early thirties, I saw
that I was a speck of light in the great
river of light that undulates through time.

I was floating with the whole
human family. We were all colors – those
who are living now, those who have died,
those who are not yet born. For a few

moments I floated, completely calm,
and I no longer hated having to exist.

Like a crow who smells hot blood
you came flying to pull me out

of the glowing stream.
'I'll hold you up. I never let my dear
ones drown!' After that, I wept for days.

6 *In and Out*

The dog searches until he finds me
upstairs, lies down with a clatter
of elbows, puts his head on my foot.

Sometimes the sound of his breathing
saves my life – in and out, in
and out; a pause, a long sigh....

7 *Pardon*

A piece of burned meat
wears my clothes, speaks
in my voice, dispatches obligations
haltingly, or not at all.
It is tired of trying
to be stouthearted, tired
beyond measure.

We move on to the monoamine
oxidase inhibitors. Day and night
I feel as if I had drunk six cups
of coffee, but the pain stops
abruptly. With the wonder
and bitterness of someone pardoned
for a crime she did not commit
I come back to marriage and friends,
to pink-fringed hollyhocks; come back
to my desk, books, and chair.

8 *Credo*

Pharmaceutical wonders are at work
but I believe only in this moment
of well-being. Unholy ghost,
you are certain to come again.

Coarse, mean, you'll put your feet
on the coffee table, lean back,
and turn me into someone who can't
take the trouble to speak; someone
who can't sleep, or who does nothing
but sleep; can't read, or call
for an appointment for help.

There is nothing I can do
against your coming.
When I awake, I am still with thee.

9 *Wood Thrush*

High on Nardil and June light
I wake at four,
waiting greedily for the first
notes of the wood thrush. Easeful air
presses through the screen
with the wild, complex song
of the bird, and I am overcome

by ordinary contentment.
What hurt me so terribly
all my life until this moment?
How I love the small, swiftly
beating heart of the bird
singing in the great maples;
its bright, unequivocal eye.

Chrysanthemums

The doctor averted his eyes
while the diagnosis fell on us,
as though the picture of the girl
hiding from her dog
had suddenly fallen off the wall.
We were speechless all the way home.
The light seemed strange.

A weekend of fear and purging....
Determined to work, he packed his
Dictaphone, a stack of letters,
and a roll of stamps. At last the day
of scalpels, blood, and gauze arrived.

Eyes closed, I lay on his tightly made
bed, waiting. From the hallway I heard
an old man, whose nurse was helping him
to walk: 'That Howard Johnson's. It's
nothing but the same thing over and over
again.'
          'That's right. It's nothing special.'

Late in the afternoon, when slanting
sun betrayed a wad of dust under the bed-
side stand, I heard the sound of casters
and footsteps slowing down.
The attendants asked me to leave the room
while they moved him onto the bed,
and the door remained closed a long time.

Evening came....
While he dozed, fitfully, still stupefied
by anesthetics, I tried to read,
my feet propped on the rails of the bed.
Odette's chrysanthemums
were revealed to me, ranks of them

in the house where Swann, jealousy
constricting his heart, made late-night calls.

And while I read, pausing again
and again to look at him, the smell
of chrysanthemums sent by friends
wavered from the sill, mixing
with the smells of drastic occasions
and disinfected sheets.

He was too out of it
to press the bolus for medication.
Every eight minutes, when he could have
more, I pressed it, and morphine dripped
from the vial in the locked box
into his arm. I made a hive
of eight-minute cells
where he could sleep without pain,
or beyond caring about pain.

Over days the IVs came out,
and freedom came back to him –
walking, shaving, sitting in a chair.
The most ordinary gestures seemed
cause for celebration.
Hazy with analgesics, he read
the *Boston Globe*, and began to talk
on the telephone.

Once the staples were out,
and we had the discharge papers
in hand, I brought him home, numbed up
for the trip. He dozed in the car,
woke, and looked with astonishment
at the hills, gold and quince
under October sun, a sight so
overwhelming that we began to cry,
he first, and then I.

Back

We try a new drug, a new combination
of drugs, and suddenly
I fall into my life again

like a vole picked up by a storm
then dropped three valleys
and two mountains away from home.

I can find my way back. I know
I will recognise the store
where I used to buy milk and gas.

I remember the house and barn,
the rake, the blue cups and plates,
the Russian novels I loved so much,

and the black silk nightgown
that he once thrust
into the toe of my Christmas stocking.

Moving the Frame

Impudent spring has come
since your chest rose and fell
for the last time, bringing
the push and ooze of budding peonies,
with ants crawling over them
exuberantly.

I have framed the picture
from your obituary. It must have been
taken on a hot graduation day:
You're wearing your academic robes
– how splendid they were –
and your hair and beard are curly
with sweat. The tassel sways....
No matter how I move your face
around my desk,
your eyes don't meet my eyes.

There was one hard night
while your breath became shallower
and shallower, and then
you were gone from us. A person
simply vanishes! I came home
and fell deeply asleep for a long
time, but I woke up again.

Winter Lambs

All night snow came upon us
with unwavering intent –
small flakes not meandering
but driving thickly down. We woke
to see the yard, the car and road
heaped unrecognisably.

The neighbors' ewes are lambing
in this stormy weather. Three
lambs born yesterday, three more
expected....
        Felix the ram looked
proprietary in his separate pen
while fatherhood accrued to him.
The panting ewes regarded me
with yellow-green, small-
pupiled eyes.

I have a friend who is pregnant –
plans gone awry – and not altogether
pleased. I don't say she should
be pleased. We are creation's
property, its particles, its clay
as we fall into this life,
agree or disagree.

Coats

I saw him leaving the hospital
with a woman's coat over his arm.
Clearly she would not need it.
The sunglasses he wore could not
conceal his wet face, his bafflement.

As if in mockery the day was fair,
and the air mild for December. All the same
he had zipped his own coat and tied
the hood under his chin, preparing
for irremediable cold.

In Memory of Jack

Once, coming down the long hill
into Andover on an autumn night
just before deer season, I stopped
the car abruptly to avoid a doe.

She stood, head down, perhaps twenty
feet away, her legs splayed
as if she meant to stand her ground.

For a long moment she looked
at the car, then bolted right at it,
glancing off the hood with a crash,
into a field of corn stubble.

So I rushed at your illness, your
suffering and death – the bright
lights of annihilation and release.

Peonies at Dusk

White peonies blooming along the porch
send out light
while the rest of the yard grows dim.

Outrageous flowers as big as human
heads! They're staggered
by their own luxuriance: I had
to prop them up with stakes and twine.

The moist air intensifies their scent,
and the moon moves around the barn
to find out what it's coming from.

In the darkening June evening
I draw a blossom near, and bending close
search it as a woman searches
a loved one's face.

Three Small Oranges

My old flannel nightgown, the elbows out,
one shoulder torn…. Instead of putting it
away with the clean wash, I cut it up
for rags, removing the arms and opening
their seams, scissoring across the breast
and upper back, then tearing the thin
cloth of the body into long rectangles.
Suddenly an immense sadness….

Making supper, I listen to news
from the war, of torture where the air
is black at noon with burning oil,
and of a market in Baghdad, bombed
by accident, where yesterday an old man
carried in his basket a piece of fish
wrapped in paper and tied with string,
and three small hard green oranges.

Potato

In haste one evening while making dinner
I threw away a potato that was spoiled
on one end. The rest would have been

redeemable. In the yellow garbage pail
it became the consort of coffee grounds,
banana skins, carrot peelings.
I pitched it onto the compost
where steaming scraps and leaves
return, like bodies over time, to earth.

When I flipped the fetid layers with a hay
fork to air the pile, the potato turned up
unfailingly, as if to revile me –

looking plumper, firmer, resurrected
instead of disassembling. It seemed to grow
until I might have made shepherd's pie
for a whole hamlet, people who pass the day
dropping trees, pumping gas, pinning
hand-me-down clothes on the line.

Gettysburg: July 1, 1863

The young man, hardly more
than a boy, who fired the shot
had looked at him with an air
not of anger but of concentration,
as if he were surveying a road,
or feeding a length of wood into a saw:
It had to be done just so.

The bullet passed through
his upper chest, below the collarbone.
The pain was not what he might
have feared. Strangely exhilarated
he staggered out of the pasture
and into a grove of trees.

He pressed and pressed
the wound, trying to stanch
the blood, but he could only press
what he could reach, and he could
not reach his back, where the bullet
had exited.
       He lay on the earth
smelling the leaves and mosses,
musty and damp and cool
after the blaze of open afternoon.

How good the earth smelled,
as it had when he was a boy
hiding from his father,
who was intent on strapping him
for doing his chores
late one time too many.

A cowbird razzed from a rail fence.
It isn't mockery, he thought,
no malice in it…just a noise.

Stray bullets nicked the oaks
overhead. Leaves and splinters fell.

Someone near him groaned.
But it was his own voice he heard.
His fingers and feet tingled,
the roof of his mouth,
and the bridge of his nose....

He became dry, dry, and thought
of Christ, who said, *I thirst.*
His man-smell, the smell of his hair
and skin, his sweat, the salt smell
of his cock and the little ferny hairs
that two women had known
left him, and a sharp, almost sweet
smell began to rise from his open mouth
in the warm shade of the oaks.
A streak of sun climbed the rough
trunk of a tree, but he did not
see it with his open eye.

Pharaoh

'The future ain't what it used to be,'
said the sage of the New York Yankees
as he pounded his mitt, releasing
the red dust of the infield
into the harshly illuminated evening air.

Big hands. Men with big hands
make things happen. The surgeon,
when I asked how big your tumor was,
held forth his substantial fist
with its globed class ring.

Home again, we live as charily as strangers.
Things are off: Touch rankles, food
is not good. Even the kindness of friends
turns burdensome; their flowers sadden
us, so many and so fair.

I woke in the night to see your
diminished bulk lying beside me –
you on your back, like a sarcophagus
as your feet held up the covers....
The things you might need in the next
life surrounded you – your comb and glasses,
water, a book and a pen.

Otherwise

I got out of bed
on two strong legs.
It might have been
otherwise. I ate
cereal, sweet
milk, ripe, flawless
peach. It might
have been otherwise.
I took the dog uphill
to the birch wood.
All morning I did
the work I love.

At noon I lay down
with my mate. It might
have been otherwise.
We ate dinner together
at a table with silver
candlesticks. It might
have been otherwise.
I slept in a bed
in a room with paintings
on the walls, and
planned another day
just like this day.
But one day, I know,
it will be otherwise.

Notes from the Other Side

I divested myself of despair
and fear when I came here.

Now there is no more catching
one's own eye in the mirror,

there are no bad books, no plastic,
no insurance premiums, and of course

no illness. Contrition
does not exist, nor gnashing

of teeth. No one howls as the first
clod of earth hits the casket.

The poor we no longer have with us.
Our calm hearts strike only the hour,

and God, as promised, proves
to be mercy clothed in light.

new poems from

OTHERWISE

(1996)

Happiness

There's just no accounting for happiness,
or the way it turns up like a prodigal
who comes back to the dust at your feet
having squandered a fortune far away.

And how can you not forgive?
You make a feast in honor of what
was lost, and take from its place the finest
garment, which you saved for an occasion
you could not imagine, and you weep night and day
to know that you were not abandoned,
that happiness saved its most extreme form
for you alone.

No, happiness is the uncle you never
knew about, who flies a single-engine plane
onto the grassy landing strip, hitchhikes
into town, and inquires at every door
until he finds you asleep midafternoon
as you so often are during the unmerciful
hours of your despair.

It comes to the monk in his cell.
It comes to the woman sweeping the street
with a birch broom, to the child
whose mother has passed out from drink.
It comes to the lover, to the dog chewing
a sock, to the pusher, to the basket maker,

and to the clerk stacking cans of carrots
in the night.
            It even comes to the boulder
in the perpetual shade of pine barrens,
to rain falling on the open sea,
to the wineglass, weary of holding wine.

Mosaic of the Nativity: Serbia, Winter 1993

On the domed ceiling God
is thinking:
I made them my joy,
and everything else I created
I made to bless them.
But see what they do!
I know their hearts
and arguments:

'We're descended from
Cain. Evil is nothing new,
so what does it matter now
if we shell the infirmary,
and the well where the fearful
and rash alike must
come for water?'

God thinks Mary into being.
Suspended at the apogee
of the golden dome,
she curls in a brown pod,
and inside her the mind
of Christ, cloaked in blood,
lodges and begins to grow.

Man Eating

The man at the table across from mine
is eating yogurt. His eyes, following
the progress of the spoon, cross briefly
each time it nears his face. Time,

and the world with all its principalities,
might come to an end as prophesied
by the Apostle John, but what about
this man, so completely present

to the little carton with its cool,
sweet food, which has caused no animal
to suffer, and which he is eating
with a pearl-white plastic spoon.

Cesarean

The surgeon with his unapologetic
blade parted darkness, revealing
day. Then from her large clay
he drew toward his masked
face my small clay. The clatter,
the white light, the vast freedom
were terrible. Outside in, oh, inside
out, and why did everybody shout?

Surprise

He suggests pancakes at the local diner,
followed by a walk in search of mayflowers,
while friends convene at the house
bearing casseroles and a cake, their cars
pulled close along the sandy shoulders
of the road, where tender ferns unfurl
in the ditches, and this year's budding leaves
push last year's spectral leaves from the tips
of the twigs of the ash trees. The gathering
itself is not what astounds her, but the casual
accomplishment with which he has lied.

No

The last prayer had been said,
and it was time to turn away
from the casket, poised on its silver
scaffolding over the open hole
that smelled like a harrowed field.
And then I heard a noise that seemed
not to be human. It was more like wind
among leafless trees, or cattle lowing
in a distant barn. I paused with one
hand on the roof of the car,
while the sound rose in pitch, then
cohered into language: *No, don't do this
to me! No, no...!* And each of us
stood where we were, unsure
whether to stay, or leave her there.

In the Nursing Home

She is like a horse grazing
a hill pasture that someone makes
smaller by coming every night
to pull the fences in and in.

She has stopped running wide loops,
stopped even the tight circles.
She drops her head to feed; grass
is dust, and the creekbed's dry.

Master, come with your light
halter. Come and bring her in.

How Like the Sound

How like the sound of laughing weeping
is. I wasn't sure until I saw your face –
your eyes squeezed shut, and the big
hot tears spurting out.

There you sat, upright, in your mother's
reclining chair, tattered from the wear
of many years. Not since childhood
had you wept this way, head back, throat

open like a hound. Of course the howling
had to stop. I saw you add *call realtor*
to your list before your red face
vanished behind the morning *Register*.

Eating the Cookies

The cousin from Maine, knowing
about her diverticulitis, left out the nuts,
so the cookies weren't entirely to my taste,
but they were good enough; yes, good enough.

Each time I emptied a drawer or shelf
I permitted myself to eat one.
I cleared the closet of silk caftans
that slipped easily from clattering hangers,
and from the bureau I took her nightgowns
and sweaters, financial documents
neatly cinctured in long gray envelopes,
and the hairnets and peppermints she'd tucked among
Lucite frames abounding with great-grandchildren,
solemn in their Christmas finery.

Finally the drawers were empty,
the bags full, and the largest cookie,
which I had saved for last, lay
solitary in the tin with a nimbus
of crumbs around it. There would be no more
parcels from Portland. I took it up
and sniffed it, and before eating it,
pressed it against my forehead, because
it seemed like the next thing to do.

Prognosis

I walked alone in the chill of dawn
while my mind leapt, as the teachers

of detachment say, like a drunken
monkey. Then a gray shape, an owl,

passed overhead. An owl is not
like a crow. A crow makes convivial

chuckings as it flies,
but the owl flew well beyond me

before I heard it coming, and when it
settled, the bough did not sway.

Afternoon at MacDowell

On a windy summer day the well-dressed
trustees occupy the first row
under the yellow and white striped canopy.
Their drive for capital is over,
and for a while this refuge is secure.

Thin after your second surgery, you wear
the gray summer suit we bought eight
years ago for momentous occasions
in warm weather. My hands rest in my lap,
under the fine cotton shawl embroidered
with mirrors that we bargained for last fall
in Bombay, unaware of your sickness.

The legs of our chairs poke holes
in the lawn. The sun goes in and out
of the grand clouds, making the air alive
with golden light, and then, as if heaven's
spirits had fallen, everything's somber again.

After music and poetry we walk to the car.
I believe in the miracles of art, but what
prodigy will keep you safe beside me,
fumbling with the radio while you drive
to find late innings of a Red Sox game?

Fat

The doctor says it's better for my spine
this way – more fat, more estrogen.
Well, then! There was a time when a wife's
plump shoulders signified prosperity.

These days my fashionable friends
get by on seaweed milkshakes,
Pall Malls, and vitamin pills. Their clothes
hang elegantly from their clavicles.

As the evening news makes clear
the starving and the besieged maintain
the current standard of beauty without effort.

Whenever two or three gather together
the talk turns dreamily to sausages,
purple cabbages, black beans and rice,
noodles gleaming with cream, yams, and plums,
and chapati fried in ghee.

Dutch Interiors

(for Caroline)

Christ has been done to death
in the cold reaches of northern Europe
a thousand thousand times.
                     Suddenly bread
and cheese appear on a plate
beside a gleaming pewter beaker of beer.
Now tell me that the Holy Ghost
does not reside in the play of light
on cutlery!

A woman makes lace,
with a moist-eyed spaniel lying
at her small shapely feet.
Even the maid with the chamber pot
is here; the naughty, red-cheeked girl....

And the merchant's wife, still
in her yellow dressing gown
at noon, dips her quill into India ink
with an air of cautious pleasure.

Reading Aloud to My Father

I chose the book haphazard
from the shelf, but with Nabokov's first
sentence I knew it wasn't the thing
to read to a dying man:
The cradle rocks above an abyss, it began,
and common sense tells us that our existence
is but a brief crack of light
between two eternities of darkness.

The words disturbed both of us immediately,
and I stopped. With music it was the same –
Chopin's Piano Concerto – he asked me
to turn it off. He ceased eating, and drank
little, while the tumors briskly appropriated
what was left of him.

But to return to the cradle rocking. I think
Nabokov had it wrong. This is the abyss.
That's why babies howl at birth,
and why the dying so often reach
for something only they can apprehend.

At the end they don't want their hands
to be under the covers, and if you should put
your hand on theirs in a tentative gesture
of solidarity, they'll pull the hand free;
and you must honor that desire,
and let them pull it free.

Woman, Why Are You Weeping?

The morning after the crucifixion,
Mary Magdalene came to see the body
of Christ. She found the stone
rolled away from an empty tomb. Two
figures dressed in white asked her,
'Woman, why are you weeping?'

'Because,' she replied, 'they have
taken away my Lord, and I don't know
where they have laid him.'

Returned from long travel, I sit
in the familiar, sun-streaked pew, waiting
for the bread and wine of Holy Communion.
The old comfort does not rise in me, only
apathy and bafflement.
                          India, with her ceaseless
bells and fire; her crows calling stridently
all night; India with her sandalwood
smoke, and graceful gods, many-headed and many-
armed, has taken away the one who blessed
and kept me.
                The thing is done, as surely
as if my luggage had been stolen from the train.
Men and women with faces as calm as lakes at dusk
have taken away my Lord, and I don't know
where to find him.

                          *

What is Brahman? I don't know Brahman.
I don't know *saccidandana*, the bliss
of the absolute and unknowable.
I only know that I have lost the Lord
in whose image I was made.

140

Whom shall I thank for this pear,
sweet and white? Food is God, *Prasadam*,
God's mercy. But who is this God?
The one who is *not this, not that*?

The absurdity of all religious forms
breaks over me, as the absurdity of language
made me feel faint the day I heard friends
giving commands to their neighbor's dog
in Spanish.... At first I laughed,
but then I became frightened.

*

They have taken away my Lord, a person
whose life I held inside me. I saw him
heal, and teach, and eat among sinners.
I saw him break the sabbath to make a higher
sabbath. I saw him lose his temper.

I knew his anguish when he called, 'I thirst!'
and received vinegar to drink. The Bible
does not say it, but I am sure he turned
his head away. Not long after he cried, 'My God,
my God, why have you forsaken me?'

I watched him reveal himself risen
to Magdalene with a single word: 'Mary!'

It was my habit to speak to him. His goodness
perfumed my life. I loved the Lord, he heard
my cry, and he loved me as his own.

*

A man sleeps on the pavement, on a raffia mat –
the only thing that has not been stolen from him.
This stranger who loves what cannot be understood
has put out my light with his calm face.

Shall the fire answer my fears and vapors?
The fire cares nothing for my illness,
nor does Brahma, the creator, nor Shiva who sees
evil with his terrible third eye; Vishnu,
the protector, does not protect me.

I've brought home the smell of the streets
in the folds of soft, bright cotton garments.
When I iron them the steam beings back
the complex odors that rise from the gutters,
of tuberoses, urine, dust, joss, and death.

*

On a curb in Allahabad the family gathers
under a dusty tree, a few quilts hung
between lightposts and a wattle fence
for privacy. Eleven sit or lie around the fire
while a woman of sixty stirs a huge pot.
Rice cooks in a narrow-necked crock
on the embers. A small dog, with patches of bald,
red skin on his back, lies on the corner
of the piece of canvas that serves as flooring.

Looking at them I lose my place.
I don't know why I was born, or why
I live in a house in New England, or why I am
a visitor with heavy luggage giving lectures
for the State Department. Why am I not
tap-tapping with my fingernail
on the rolled-up window of a white Government car,
a baby in my arms, drugged to look feverish?

*

Rajiv did not weep. He did not cover
his face with his hands when we rowed past
the dead body of a newborn nudging the grassy
banks at Benares – close by a snake
rearing up, and a cast-off garland of flowers.

He explained. When a family are too poor
to cremate their dead, they bring the body
here, and slip it into the waters of the Ganges
and Yamuna rivers.
                    Perhaps the child was dead
at birth; perhaps it had the misfortune
to be born a girl. The mother may have walked
two days with her baby's body to this place
where Gandhi's ashes once struck the waves
with a sound like gravel being scuffed
over the edge of a bridge.

'What shall we do about this?' I asked
my God, who even then was leaving me. The reply
was scorching wind, lapping of water, pull
of the black oarsmen on the oars....

The Sick Wife

The sick wife stayed in the car
while he bought a few groceries.
Not yet fifty,
she had learned what it's like
not to be able to button a button.

It was the middle of the day –
and so only mothers with small children
or retired couples
stepped though the muddy parking lot.

Dry cleaning swung and gleamed on hangers
in the cars of the prosperous.
How easily they moved –
with such freedom,
even the old and relatively infirm.

The windows began to steam up.
The cars on either side of her
pulled away so briskly
that it made her sick at heart.

TWENTY POEMS OF
ANNA AKHMATOVA

(1985)

translated from the Russian by
JANE KENYON
with
VERA SANDOMIRSKY DUNHAM

INTRODUCTION

As we remember Keats for the beauty and intensity of his shorter poems, especially the odes and sonnets, so we revere Akhmatova for her early lyrics – brief, perfectly made verses of passion and feeling. Images build emotional pressure:

> And sweeter even than the singing of songs
> is this dream, now becoming real:
> the swaying of branches brushed aside
> and the faint ringing of your spurs.

I love the sudden twists these poems take, often in the last line. In one poem the recollection of a literary party ends with the first frank exchange of glances between lovers. Another poem lists sweet-smelling things – mignonette, violets, apples – and ends, astonishingly, '...we have found out forever / that blood smells only of blood.' These poems celebrate the sensual life, and Akhmatova's devoted attention to details of sense always serves feeling:

> With the hissing of a snake the scythe cuts down
> the stalks, one pressed hard against another.

The snake's hissing is accurate to the sound of scythe mowing, and more than accurate: by using the snake for her auditory image, Akhmatova compares this rural place, where love has gone awry, to the lost Eden.

Akhmatova was born Anna Gorenko near Odessa in 1889. Soon her family moved to Tsarskoe Selo, near St Petersburg, and there she began her education. Studying French, she learned to love Baudelaire and Verlaine. At the age of ten she became seriously ill, with a disease never diagnosed, and went deaf for a brief time. As she recovered she wrote her first poems.

Money was not abundant in the Gorenko household, nor was tranquility. Akhmatova did not get on with her father, Andrei Gorenko, a naval engineer who lectured at the Naval Academy in St Petersburg – also a notorious philanderer whose money went to his mistresses. (We know little of Akhmatova's relationship with her mother.) Akhmatova's brother Victor recalls an occasion when the young girl asked their father for money for a new coat. When he refused she threw off her clothes and became hysterical. (See *Akhmatova: Poems, Correspondence, Reminiscences, Iconography*: Ardis.) Andrei Gorenko deserted his family in 1905. A few years later, hearing that his daughter wrote verse, he asked her to choose a pen name. He wished to avoid the ignominy, as he put it, of 'a decadent poetess' in the family. She took her Tartar great-grandmother's name.

When Akhmatova was still a schoolgirl she met Nikolai Gumilev, a poet and founder of Acmeism who became her mentor and her first husband. Nadezhda Mandelstam has said that Akhmatova rarely spoke of her childhood; she seemed to consider her marriage to Gumilev the beginning of her life. (See Nadezhda Mandelstam's *Hope Abandoned*.) She was slow to accept his proposal. He sought her attention by repeated attempts at suicide until she finally married him in 1910. The bride's family did not attend the ceremony. Having won her at last, Gumilev promptly left to spend six months in Africa. On his return, while still at the train station, he asked her if she had been writing. By reply she handed him the manuscript of *Evening*, her first book.

Their son, Lev Gumilev, was born in 1912, the same year Akhmatova published *Evening*. By 1917, when she was 28, she had brought out two more books, *Rosary* and *White Flock*. Despite the historical tumult of World War I and the Revolution, her poetry quickly became popular. But tumult was private as well as public: by 1918 her marriage had failed; Akhmatova divorced Gumilev and the same autumn married the Assyriologist V.K. Shileiko. This unhappy alliance – Shileiko burned his wife's poems in the samovar – lasted for six years. (See Amanda Haight's biography, *Akhmatova: A Poetic Pilgrimage*: Oxford.) Ordinary family life eluded Akhmatova, who went through many love affairs. Before her divorce from Shileiko, she lived in a ménage à trois with Nikolai Punin and his wife; Punin later became her third husband. Motherhood was not easy. ('The lot of a mother is a bright torture: I was not worthy of it....') For the most part, Gumilev's mother raised her grandson Lev.

In the years following her early triumphs Akhmatova suffered many torments, as the Soviet régime hardened into tyranny. Gumilev was executed in 1921 for alleged anti-Bolshevik activity. Early in the 1920s Soviet critics denounced Akhmatova's work as anachronistic and useless to the Revolution. The Central Committee of the Communist Party forbade publication of her verse; from 1923 to 1940, none of her poetry appeared in print. The great poems of her maturity, *Requiem*, and *Song Without a Hero*, exist in Russia today only by underground publication, or *samizdat*.

During the Stalinist terror of the 1930s the poet's son Lev and her husband Punin were imprisoned. Akhmatova's fellow Acmeist and close friend Osip Mandelstam died in a prison camp in 1938. (Punin died in another camp fifteen years later.) During the Second World War the Committee of the Communist Party of Leningrad evacuated Akhmatova to Tashkent in Uzbekistan. There she lived in a small, hot room, in ill health, with Osip Mandelstam's widow Nadezhda.

In 1944 Akhmatova returned to Leningrad, to a still-higher wave of official antagonism. In a prominent literary magazine, Andrei Zhdanov denounced her as '...a frantic little fine lady flitting between the boudoir and the chapel...half-nun, half-harlot'. The Union of Soviet Writers expelled her. A new book of poems, already in print, was seized and destroyed. For many years she supported herself only by working as a translator from Asiatic languages and from French, an activity she compared to 'eating one's own brain' (Haight).

The final decade of her life was relatively tranquil. During the thaw that followed Stalin's death, the government released Lev Gumilev from labor camp and reinstated Akhmatova in the Writer's Union. She was permitted to publish and to travel. In Italy and England she received honors and saw old friends. She died in March 1966, and was buried at Komarovo, near Leningrad.

Akhmatova's work ranges from the highly personal early lyrics through the longer, more public and political *Requiem*, on to the allusive and cryptic *Poem Without a Hero*. The early poems embody Acmeist principles. Acmeism grew out of the Poet's Guild, which Nikolai Gumilev and Sergei Gorodetsky founded in 1912 – fifteen poets who met regularly to read poems and argue aesthetic theory. At one meeting, Gumilev proposed an attack on Symbolism with its 'obligatory mysticism'. He proposed Acmeism as an alternative; Acmeism held that a rose is beautiful in itself, not because it stands for something. These poets announced that they were craftsmen not priests, and dedicated themselves to clarity, concision, and perfection of form. They summed up their goals in two words: 'beautiful clarity'. Gumilev himself, Akhmatova, and Osip Mandelstam were the leading Acmeists, and the movement thrived for a decade.

Written so many years later, *Requiem* and *Poem Without a Hero* naturally moved past Akhmatova's early poems in intention and in scope. They are manifestly political and historical. *Requiem* records the terror of the purges in the 1930s, commemorating the women who stood waiting outside prison gates with parcels for husbands, sons, and brothers; Akhmatova compares the suffering of these women to Mary's at the Crucifixion. In the prefatory note to *Poem Without a Hero* Akhmatova says: 'I dedicate this poem to its first listeners – my friends and countrymen who perished in Leningrad during the siege.'

These translations are free-verse versions of rhymed and metered poems. Losing the formal perfection of the Russian verses – much of the 'beautiful clarity' – has been a constant source of frustration and sadness to me and to my co-worker, Vera Sandomirsky Dunham. But something, I think, crosses the barrier between our languages. Because it is impossible to translate with fidelity to form *and* to image, I have sacrificed form for image. Image embodies feeling, and this embodiment is perhaps the greatest treasure of lyric poetry. In translating, I mean to place the integrity of the image over all other considerations.

Translation provides many frustrations. It seems impossible to translate a single Russian syllable that means 'What did he have to do that for?' Trying to translate lines about a native place – so important to Akhmatova, who firmly refused expatriation – how does one render *rodnoi*, which means 'all that is dear to me, familiar, my own...'? I remember Vera clapping her hands to her head and moaning, 'This will sink us...'

There are times when – in the interest of cadence, tone, or clarity – I have altered punctuation or moved something from one line to another. Often I needed to shift the verb from the end to the beginning of the sentence. Sometimes a word, translated from Russian as the dictionary would have it, made impossible English. I list significant variations from the original in notes at the back of this book. We have translated from the two-volume *Works*, edited by G.P. Struve and B.A. Filippov, published by Interlanguage Literary Associates in 1965.

I want to thank Robert Bly, who first encouraged me to read Akhmatova, and later to translate these poems. I also thank Lou Teel, who, as a student of Russian at Dartmouth, helped me begin the work. I owe special thanks to Vera Sandomirsky Dunham, a busy scholar, teacher, and lifelong lover of these poems. Her fear that a free-verse translation of Akhmatova is fundamentally misconceived has not prevented her from offering her time, her erudition, and her hospitality.

J.K.
[1984]

1

The memory of sun weakens in my heart,
grass turns yellow,
wind blows the early flakes of snow
lightly, lightly.

Already the narrow canals have stopped flowing;
water freezes.
Nothing will ever happen here –
not ever!

Against the empty sky the willow opens
a transparent fan.
Maybe it's a good thing I'm not
your wife.

The memory of sun weakens in my heart.
What's this? Darkness?
It's possible. And this may be the first night
of winter.

[*1911*]

2

Evening hours at the desk.
And a page irreparably white.
The mimosa calls up the heat of Nice,
a large bird flies in a beam of moonlight.

And having braided my hair carefully for the night
as if tomorrow braids will be necessary,
I look out the window, no longer sad, –
at the sea, the sandy slopes.

What power a man has
who doesn't ask for tenderness!
I cannot lift my tired eyes
when he speaks my name.

[*1913*]

3

I know, I know the skis
will begin again their dry creaking.
In the dark blue sky the moon is red,
and the meadow slopes so sweetly.

The windows of the palace burn
remote and still.
No path, no lane,
only the iceholes are dark.

Willow, tree of nymphs,
don't get in my way.
Shelter the black grackles, black
grackles among your snowy branches.

[*1913*]

4 *The Guest*

Everything's just as it was: fine hard snow
beats against the dining room windows,
and I myself have not changed:
even so, a man came to call.

I asked him: 'What do you want?'
He said, 'To be with you in hell.'
I laughed: 'It seems you see
plenty of trouble ahead for us both.'

But lifting his dry hand
he lightly touched the flowers.
'Tell me how they kiss you,
tell me how you kiss.'

And his half-closed eyes
remained on my ring.
Not even the smallest muscle moved
in his serenely angry face.

Oh, I know it fills him with joy –
this hard and passionate certainty
that there is nothing he needs,
and nothing I can keep from him.

[*1 January 1914*]

5

(N.V.N.)

There is a sacred, secret line in loving
which attraction and even passion cannot cross, –
even if lips draw near in awful silence
and love tears at the heart.

Friendship is weak and useless here,
and years of happiness, exalted and full of fire,
because the soul is free and does not know
the slow luxuries of sensual life.

Those who try to come near it are insane
and those who reach it are shaken by grief.
So now you know exactly why
my heart beats no faster under your hand.

[*1915*]

6

Like a white stone in a deep well
one memory lies inside me.
I cannot and will not fight against it:
it is joy and it is pain.

It seems to me that anyone who looks
into my eyes will notice it immediately,
becoming sadder and more pensive
than someone listening to a melancholy tale.

I remember how the gods turned people
into things, not killing their consciousness.
And now, to keep these glorious sorrows alive,
you have turned into my memory of you.

[*1916, Slepnevo*]

7

Everything promised him to me:
the fading amber edge of the sky,
and the sweet dreams of Christmas,
and the wind at Easter, loud with bells,

and the red shoots of the grapevine,
and waterfalls in the park,
and two large dragonflies
on the rusty iron fencepost.

And I could only believe
that he would be mine
as I walked along the high slopes,
the path of burning stones.

[*1916*]

8

Yes I loved them, those gatherings late at night, –
the small table, glasses with frosted sides,
fragrant vapor rising from black coffee,
the fireplace, red with powerful winter heat,
the biting gaiety of a literary joke,
and the first helpless and frightening glance of my love.

[*1917*]

9

Twenty-first. Night. Monday.
Silhouette of the capitol in darkness.
Some good-for-nothing – who knows why –
made up the tale that love exists on earth.

People believe it, maybe from laziness
or boredom, and live accordingly:
they wait eagerly for meetings, fear parting,
and when they sing, they sing about love.

But the secret reveals itself to some,
and on them silence settles down...
I found this out by accident
and now it seems I'm sick all the time.

[*1917*]

10

There is a certain hour every day
so troubled and heavy...
I speak to melancholy in a loud voice
not bothering to open my sleepy eyes.
And it pulses like blood,
is warm like a sigh,
like happy love
is smart and nasty.

[*1917*]

11

We walk along the hard crest of the snowdrift
toward my white, mysterious house,
both of us so quiet,
keeping the silence as we go along.
And sweeter even than the singing of songs
is this dream, now becoming real:
the swaying of branches brushed aside
and the faint ringing of your spurs.

[*January 1917*]

12

All day the crowd rushes one way, then another;
its own gasping frightens it still more,
and laughing skulls fly on funereal banners,
prophesying from the river's far side.
For this I sang and dreamed!
They have torn my heart in two.
How quiet it is after the volley!
Death sends patrols into every courtyard.

[*1917*]

13

The river flows without hurry through the valley,
a house with many windows rises on the hill –
and we live as people did under Catherine;
hold church services at home, wait for harvest.
Two days have passed, two days' separation;
a guest comes riding along a golden wheatfield.
In the parlor he kisses my grandmother's hand,
and on the steep staircase he kisses my lips.

[*Summer 1917*]

14

The mysterious spring still lay under a spell,
the transparent wind stalked over the mountains,
and the deep lake kept on being blue, –
a temple of the Baptist not made by hands.

You were frightened by our first meeting,
but I already prayed for the second, and now
the evening is hot, the way it was then...
How close the sun has come to the mountain.

You are not with me, but this is no separation:
to me each instant is – triumphant news.
I know there is such anguish in you
that you cannot say a single word.

[*Spring 1917*]

15

I hear the always-sad voice of the oriole
and I salute the passing of delectable summer.
With the hissing of a snake the scythe cuts down
the stalks, one pressed hard against another.

And the hitched-up skirts of the slender reapers
fly in the wind like holiday flags. Now if only
we had the cheerful ring of harness bells,
a lingering glance through dusty eyelashes.

I don't expect caresses or flattering love-talk,
I sense unavoidable darkness coming near,
but come and see the Paradise where together,
blissful and innocent, we once lived.

[*1917*]

16

You are an apostate: for a green island
you give away your native land,
our songs and our icons
and the pine tree over the quiet lake.

Why is it, you dashing man from Yaroslav,
if you still have your wits
why are you gaping at the beautiful redheads
and the luxurious houses?

You might as well be sacrilegious and swagger,
finish off your orthodox soul,
stay where you are in the royal capital
and begin to love your freedom in earnest.

How does it happen that you come to moan
under my small high window?
You know yourself that waves won't drown you
and mortal combat leaves you without a scratch.

It's true that neither the sea nor battles
frighten those who have renounced Paradise.
That's why at the hour of prayer
you asked to be remembered.

[*1917, Slepnevo*]

17

Wild honey has the scent of freedom,
dust – of a ray of sun,
a girl's mouth – of a violet,
and gold – has no perfume.

Watery – the mignonette,
and like an apple – love,
but we have found out forever
that blood smells only of blood.

18

It is not with the lyre of someone in love
that I go seducing people.
The rattle of the leper
is what sings in my hands.

19 *Tale of the Black Ring*

1

Presents were rare things
coming from my grandmother, a Tartar;
and she was bitterly angry
when I was baptised.
But she turned kind before she died
and for the first time pitied me,
sighing: 'Oh the years!
and here my young granddaughter!'
Forgiving my peculiar ways
she left her black ring to me.
She said: 'It becomes her,
with this things will be better for her.'

2

I said to my friends:
'There is plenty of grief, so little joy.'
And I left, covering my face;
I lost the ring.
My friends said:
'We looked everywhere for the ring,
on the sandy shore,
and among pines near the small clearing.'
One more daring than the rest
caught up with me on the tree-lined drive
and tried to convince me
to wait for the close of day.
The advice astonished me
and I grew angry with my friend
because his eyes were full of sympathy:
'And what do I need you for?
You can only laugh,
boast in front of the others
and bring flowers.'
I told them all to go away.

3

Coming into my cheerful room
I called out like a bird of prey,
fell back on the bed
to remember for the hundredth time
how I sat at supper
and looked into dark eyes,
ate nothing, drank nothing
at the oak table,
how under the regular pattern of the tablecloth
I held out the black ring,
how he looked into my face,
stood up and stepped out onto the porch.

. . . .

They won't come to me with what they have found!
Far over the swiftly moving boat
the sails turned white,
the sky flushed pink.

[*1917-1936*]

20 *On the Road*

Though this land is not my own
I will never forget it,
or the waters of its ocean,
fresh and delicately icy.

Sand on the bottom is whiter than chalk,
and the air drunk, like wine.
Late sun lays bare
the rosy limbs of the pine trees.

And the sun goes down in waves of ether
in such a way that I can't tell
if the day is ending, or the world,
or if the secret of secrets is within me again.

[*1964*]

APPENDICES

Everything I Know About Writing Poetry
(Notes for a Lecture)

1. Why do we want to write poems? What is behind this crazy impulse? The wish to connect with others, on a deep level, about inward things.

The pressure of emotion, which many people prefer to ignore, but which, for you, is the very substance of your work, your clay.

There's play involved in the writing of poetry. Baby waking up. We have to be like babies waking up – trying every sound, every pitch, every word, however nonsensical. Later, be a revising adult. Babies build it up and knock it down again.

There's the need to make sense of life behind the impulse to write.

And finally, we celebrate the world by writing about it, we observe it more closely, with more love. We are more fully alive and aware because of our efforts.

2. So where do we begin. We feel this pressure of emotion and thought, and we need to find, among the many things of this world, a way to *body forth* our feeling. It's metaphor, the engine of poetry, that does the work for us. Metaphor is simply talking about one thing in terms of another. Take any Robert Frost poem.

> Two roads diverged in a yellow wood
> And sorry I could not travel both
> And be one traveler, long I stood
> And looked down one as far as I could
> To where it bent in the undergrowth...

Two divergences, an inner and an outer. The thing – the image – does the work of carrying feeling. Ezra Pound once said, 'The natural object is always the adequate symbol.' Believe it, act on it, and your poems will not fly off into abstraction. A few more examples of the working image, what Eliot called the 'objective correlative' – that is, an outward sign of an inward state.

> The hare limp'd trembling through the frozen grass.
>
> KEATS: 'Eve of St Agnes'

I put my left glove on my right hand...

AKHMATOVA: 'Song of the Last Meeting'

By the gate now, the moss is grown, the different mosses
Too deep to clear them away!

POUND'S TR.: 'The River Merchant's Wife'

I want to read a couple of perfectly realised poems – perfectly
imagined – poems in which the inner world is revealed in terms of
the outer world – revealed in terms of things. The natural object
is always...

[Here Jane read aloud Elizabeth Bishop's 'Crusoe in England' and Ezra
Pound's translation 'The River Merchant's Wife: A Letter']

3. Find fresh language. Snow blanketed the field. Not good enough.
Pound said, 'Make it new.' Make it specific rather than general.
Don't say there were a few things on the desk when you can say
there were three letters on the desk, one opened in haste without
a letter opener... You cannot do without a thesaurus. The word
comes from the Latin meaning treasure. Also an OED.

3a. Omit useless words.

4. Tell the whole truth. Don't be lazy, don't be afraid. Close the
critic out when you are drafting something new. Take chances in
the interest of clarity of emotion.

5. The 'so what' test.

6. Revise.

7. Develop a tough snout. Even established writers get rejected all
the time.

8. Be a good steward of your gifts. Protect your time. Feed your
inner life. Avoid too much noise. Read good books, have good
sentences in your ears. Be by yourself as often as you can. Walk.
Take the phone off the hook. Work regular hours.

[1991]

167

from An Interview with David Bradt

BRADT: We assume that poetry matters. Why does it matter?

KENYON: It matters because it's beautiful. It matters because it tells the truth, the human truth about the complexity of life. As Akhmatova says, 'It is joy and it is pain.' It tells the entire truth about what it is to be alive, about the way of the world, about life and death. Art embodies that complexity and makes it more understandable, less frightening, less bewildering. It matters because it is consolation in times of trouble. Even when a poem addresses a painful subject, it still manages to be consoling, somehow, if it's a good poem. Poetry has an unearthly ability to turn suffering into beauty. When Don was recuperating I had Elizabeth Bishop's poems with me, and I would disappear into that book for minutes at a time, go into that world, and it was a safe place, and a very interesting place. Someone with a marvelous mind and spirit inhabits those poems.

BRADT: You've been called a contemplative poet and compared to Emily Dickinson. How do you respond to those comments?

KENYON: To be mentioned in the same breath with Emily Dickinson makes my day. If by contemplative you mean one who mediates on religious matters, I guess we both do that in our work. Dickinson thinks a lot about her soul, and I think a lot about mine. She thinks about her relation to God – a God who is distant, and rather cruelly arbitrary. In many of my poems I am searching, clumsily, for God. We are both full of terror, finally, and puzzlement, at the creation.

BRADT: What is the source of your poems? Where do they come from?

KENYON: They come from a number of sources. Finally, I guess I do not exactly know. I would say that poetry comes partly from having had a fair amount of solitude in my childhood. I grew up in the country outside Ann Arbor, Michigan. We didn't have many neighbors, and the neighbors we had didn't have kids, so I turned inward at a fairly early age. That probably has more to do with my being a poet than almost anything else. That, and the fact that when I was first introduced to poetry, which was not till I was in junior high school, I was terribly drawn by the strong emotions that I could see were the stuff of poetry. It was okay to have strong emotions in poetry. I had a lot of emotions as a child – and still have as an adult – that are pretty frightening to me. I found that poets are not afraid of feeling. That's what poetry is about; that's really the great subject of poetry. Right away I recognised poetry as a safe haven.

So where do poems come from? Primarily, I think, from childhood. That's when I fell under the thrall of nature. I spent long hours playing at the stream that ran through my family's property. We lived on a dirt road near the Huron River, across from a working farm. I fell in love with the natural world when I was a kid, so my poems are full of the natural world. I use it again and again as a way of talking about something inward. If you read my poems you would not know you were in the 20th century, because there are no airplanes or computers or e-mail.

BRADT: At what point in the making of a poem do formal concerns, like lineation, stanzas, come into play?

KENYON: Virtually from the beginning. If I showed you a poem with all of its drafts, you could see for yourself how the language changes, how the poem grows and comes into focus, pulls together. At first it's a kind of blind activity. Things come to me when I'm in a certain frame of mind. I sometimes have the feeling that I'm taking dictation. Words suggest themselves. Sometimes I'm not entirely sure of their meaning myself, so I look them up and find that maybe on some deep level I *did* know what that word means, and it just happens to be the *perfect* word. There's a tremendous sense, when I'm working well, that I'm getting a big boost from somewhere. I couldn't tell you where.

BRADT: May Sarton says that poets are chosen.

KENYON: It's pretty weird. I didn't choose poetry really. It seems to be the only thing I'm fit to do. I could be a landscape gardener if I needed to have a job in some other realm. They're both art, both arranging and rearranging things. Almost always if I search I can find something in the natural world – an objective correlative in Eliot's phrase – that embodies what I'm feeling at the moment. That's when a poem really takes off. For instance, I wrote a poem recently called 'Coats', in which I'm going into Dartmouth Hitchcock Hospital and a man is coming out of the hospital with a distraught look on his face, carrying a woman's coat over his arm. I see that, and I know what's happened. That poem threw itself at my feet: 'Write me! Write me!' I found that by talking about the coats – the man's coat and the woman's coat – I was able to write the poem. I made up the part about the man's coat in this poem. I say that even though the day was warm, he had zipped his own coat and tied the hood under his chin, 'as if preparing for irremediable cold'. It's only three stanzas long, about twelve lines, and it's all about the coats. Maybe he was taking his wife's coat to the cleaner. I doubt it; the emotional truth for me was that he had lost his wife. Lots of people would walk past that man without seeing his situation. I couldn't help seeing it!

BRADT: Who are the writers you go back to for enjoyment and perhaps for inspiration?

KENYON: I've been most excited about John Keats, Anna Akhmatova, Elizabeth Bishop, Robert Lowell, Geoffrey Hill, and Anton Chekhov. I mention Chekhov last, but he really belongs at the head of the list, oddly enough. His compassion, his delicate humor, and his profundity seem to me most enviable. And of course his brilliant use of physical detail.

BRADT: How did you become interested in Akhmatova?

KENYON: Fourteen or fifteen years ago, Don's old friend Robert Bly was visiting. As he always does he asked me what I was working on. I showed him some poems that I had been working on, and he read them thoughtfully, then looked up and said, 'It's time for you now to take a writer and work with that writer as a master.' I wasn't even sure what he meant, but I said, 'I can't have a man as a master.' He said without missing a beat, 'Then read Akhmatova.' So I began collecting translations of Akhmatova, and I found, much to my dismay, that I didn't think any of the translations were good. So as a kind of exercise in close reading I began collecting all the versions I could of a given poem, and then attempting to write my own version. That's how the door opened.

After I had been doing this for a while, I wondered if these "versions" had any real accuracy. I met a young woman at a party who was a Russian student at Dartmouth. I told her what I had been doing, and she agreed to read them for me. Lou Teel and I began working together and I began to bring the translations closer and closer to the originals. Then Robert came back for another visit. I showed him my translations and he said, 'I want to do a book of these' – for the Eighties Press. So that's how it happened.

BRADT: So you had some help with literal translation?

KENYON: Yes. After Robert told me he wanted to do the book, he said that there was one Russian scholar he wanted me to work with – Vera Sandomirsky Dunham, an émigrée and a very literary person who knows all the subtleties of both languages. Both he and Louis Simpson prevailed on Vera to work with me, and then the project really got underway. Over the next five years I made periodic trips to Vera's home on Long Island and we worked together. In working on the translations I became so close to those poems that I forgot they weren't mine. It was only after I got that close that I could feel a bit of freedom in translation. Translation is a necessary evil, and especially difficult if you are uncomfortable with the notion of compromise.

BRADT: My favorite observation on translation is Willard Trask's. Someone commented to him that translation is impossible, and he said, 'Of course. That's why I do it.' It takes a lot of nerve.

KENYON: It's a solemn pledge. You want to be as accurate as possible, but sometimes you have to change literal details to tell the emotional truth of the poem. You can get weak knees, and I think you should. Translation is an uncomfortable business. I struggled with Akhmatova, struggled not to change her images in particular. Then I would turn to my own poems with this tremendous sense of freedom, and I began to feel some power in my own work for the first time – I'm sure as a direct result of working with those translations. Now in my own work, I saw that there was nothing to limit me but my own imagination. Robert had told me that if I worked on translations they would repay me ten times over for the effort I put into them, and I thought *Yeah*. But I really got going in my own work after I did these translations. I know that if I had not worked so hard on Akhmatova I would never have experienced that surge of power. It was very exciting, and I wrote most of the poems in *The Boat of Quiet Hours* in the years during and right after I had been working on the translations.

BRADT: To what extent is sound important in translation, do you think?

KENYON: It is important. My translations were free-verse translations of rhymed and metered poems, and a lot of people would get off the bus right there. They would say, 'You've already lost a good part of what makes the poem wonderful.' That's why I say translation is a necessary evil. Either you sacrifice the sound patterns in order to keep the images intact or you sacrifice the images in order to keep the sound intact.

BRADT: Sometimes you can do both in isolated moments.

KENYON: It's rare when you can. You're going to sacrifice either image, or form and sound, and of the two the one I would be most reluctant to lose is the integrity of the images. The images in a good poem come from a deep place, and they give the poem a sense of cohesion. Almost everything else can be tinkered with, but if that is tinkered with, the whole work flies apart. Again and again I saw translations of these poems that had no respect for their psychic wholeness. The translators might have been fairly clever at their rhymes, but it was word games, not poetry. I came to believe in the absolute value of the image when I was working on these poems by Akhmatova. In one of her poems, talking about parting from a lover with whom she's had a spat, she says, 'The glove that belongs on my right hand I put on my left hand.' Can't you see this flustered, red-faced, confused, frightened woman with a wild look on her face? It's all there in that image.

BRADT: You've lived here at Eagle Pond for almost twenty years now. Have you become a poet of this place, do you think?

KENYON: Yes, I think so. I didn't really get going in my work until we came here. I have all the time in the world here. I had to do something to fill those hours, so I began to work more. I used to work only when the spirit moved, but when we came here I began to write every day, and that was a very important step for me. Inherent in that decision to work every day was the admission to myself that I was getting serious about this poetry business. It was not like learning to upholster furniture or growing plants under lights. It was something more serious.

Only two poems in all the things I've published were not written here. For one thing, living here gave me a subject. I was getting to know this place for the first time, and poetry depends a lot, I think, on the state of wonderment. Poets renew for us the awe we feel at creation. The things I noticed about this place were all subjects for poems, and I suddenly had a broad view. That was immensely important. This is such a beautiful place. It's still such an amazement that we live here among these mountains and hills. I think if Don and I had stayed in Ann Arbor and he had gone on teaching, our lives would have been very different, much more suburban and academic. Our move here permitted him to do something that he had wanted to do for a long time, to strike out on his own and go freelance, and that's precisely what he did. He was ready to do that but I think it took nudging from me to get him to do what he wanted to do. Moving here has been critical for both of us in our development as artists. This is the vale of soul-making, as Keats says. This place has made us both considerably different people. The sense of community here is something I never experienced in Ann Arbor.

BRADT: Would you describe your work habits as a writer?

KENYON: When things are going well for me, I wake early and I take the dog and go a couple of miles up Ragged Mountain. Then I come back and tidy up a bit and have breakfast and go to my study. I work all morning – on three or four poems at a time, if I'm lucky. I've found that working on one thing until it's done can make it harder to finish because if you get stuck you just have to put it down, whereas if you're working on a number of things, and you get stuck on one, you can put it down and turn to something else. After lunch, if things are really hot, I'll go back upstairs, but if not, I spend the afternoon doing chores. In gardening season I'm outdoors every day all afternoon, from June till September. I find I need that mix of sedentary work combined with something physical in the afternoon because I'm pretty restless. Holding still for a number of hours is difficult. I have the best of all worlds. When Gus and I go up on Ragged Mountain in the morning, hardly a day goes by that I don't think, *How is it that you have the phenom-enal luck to live here?*

BRADT: One of your poems speaks about plants as companions. Does your sense of companionship extend equally to animals?

KENYON: Certainly – and increasingly to plants and even stones if you want to know the truth. I see all creation as interconnected. But to get back to your question, we've had five cats in our eigh-teen years here. Gus is our first dog. I never had lived with a dog until Gus. I'm head over heels for this boy. I start every day of my life going for a run with him. He's my spiritual leader. He's entirely forgiving; he's silly; he has a wonderful sense of humor; he's earnest and hard working; he never comes back without a stick – sometimes they're five or six feet long. All the neighbors pass us on the way to work and laugh. He has an ardent nature, never discouraged. Dogs are wonderful Zen masters. He's very good at living in the present. That's an art.

I think it's important that we learn to live in the present, espe-cially if we face health problems. If we don't, we're going to wake up one day and realise the present is all we have, that's all we ever have, and we've failed to be present to the present. We all have a tendency when we're doing one thing to plan the next thing. In Bill Moyers's program on healing and the mind there's an exercise that involves eating one raisin. The natural object is always the adequate symbol. Both Don and I, days later, were still thinking about this yoga teacher eating the raisin with complete attention. When I'm gulping down a sandwich on the run because I have to go someplace or do something, that crazy raisin will come back to me and allow me to slow down. It's become a mnemonic for 'slow down'. We gulp down so much life, and it's never really ours that way. It reminds me of Christ saying in the gospels, 'He who would save his life must lose it.'

BRADT: What do you take that to mean?

KENYON: You really have to turn your complete attention to some-thing large, something that makes you forget who you are and where you are and what you have and what you don't have. You have to bring your awareness completely to this new thing.

BRADT: Suppose you were a modern-day Rilke, and let's say a Ms

175

Kappus wrote you for advice. And suppose she had at least a glimmer of talent. What would you say to her?

KENYON: I'd say that your art comes out of your life, and you have to keep living until you have enough to write about. Be patient if you can. Find friends whose judgment you trust and work with them on everything you do. Read, read, read. Art begets art, and you need to read – not just English poets but poets of other cultures and times and traditions. Don't be discouraged if the world doesn't beat a path to your door. If anyone had told me when I was beginning to write poems with serious intent, in my twenties, that it would be another ten years before I published a book, I would have said, 'I just can't take that kind of time. I'm running on a different timetable.' I think I've become more patient with the years; I'm learning to take the long view.

BRADT: Suppose Ms Kappus asked you, 'What's the poet's job?'

KENYON: The poet's job is to tell the whole truth and nothing but the truth, in such a beautiful way that people cannot live without it; to put into words those feelings we all have that are so deep, so important, and yet so difficult to name. The poet's job is to find a name for everything; to be a fearless finder of the names of things; to be an advocate for the beauty of language, the subtleties of language. I think it's very serious stuff, art; it's not just decoration. The other job the poet has is to console in the face of the inevitable disintegration of loss and death, all of the tough things we have to face as humans. We have the consolation of beauty, of one soul extending to another soul and saying, 'I've been there too.' Remember Frost's lovely little poem, about going out to clear the pasture spring? 'You come too,' he says.

[1993]

176